AT LEAST I TURN UP

The Biography of John Pullin

AT LEAST WE TURN UP

TURN UP

The Biography of John Pullin

STEVE TOMLIN

AMBERLEY

First published 2019

Amberley Publishing
The Hill, Stroud
Gloucestershire, GL5 4EP

www.amberley-books.com

British Library Cataloguing in Publication Data.
A catalogue record for this book is available from the British Library.

ISBN 978 1 4456 8075 0 (paperback)
ISBN 978 1 4456 8076 7 (ebook)

Typesetting by Aura Technology and Software Services, India.
Printed in the UK.

Contents

Foreword by Sir Gareth Edwards

I am always delighted to renew association with John Pullin, who has perhaps been something of an unsung sporting hero over the years. However, when I put together a book a few years ago about one hundred of the greatest rugby players in the history of the game, he was a natural fit who could never be left out.

I actually made my senior debut for Cardiff's second team at Bristol's Memorial Ground and although John would not have played that day, Cardiff v Bristol was always a match everyone looked forward to on both sides of the River Severn.

I had the pleasure of touring with him on two Lions tours to South Africa and New Zealand and he was always quiet, modest and unassuming with a gentle smile, but if he had something to say everyone immediately listened. He rarely sparkled around the field, preferring to concentrate his energies on his job in the set piece. Whenever I put a ball into a scrum I just knew I would immediately get it straight back for us to play with. Many hookers at the time used to moan that I used to put the ball in too fast but it never seemed to bother John in the least.

I particularly remember my first game at Twickenham against England and our captain Norman Gale kept losing the ball in the set scrums against this chap and it was frustrating the hell out of us. Mind you, we did manage to pinch just one and I was able to slip over in the corner for my first ever try for Wales!

On tour he was very much one of the 'front row union' who all loved nothing more than being around with each other clasping their pints of ale and muttering away about whatever hookers and props ever find to talk about. Later in the book you will read about the 'Wreckers' and the 'Kippers' on the 1968 Lions tour. John liked his beauty sleep and would have probably been elected the Kippers' president.

Of course, he was also an integral part of that famous try for the Barbarians against the All Blacks and people used to kid him about what he was doing standing where he was. Indeed, they said the only time he would ever take a ball under his own posts was if the opposition were kicking a conversion. I am told the front row union threatened to debar him from membership after that for being too flash!

John Pullin was a truly world-class rugby player, a delightful travelling companion, and I always look forward to seeing him again on the occasions when we meet up.

I hope you enjoy his story.

Introduction

I first met John Pullin in late 2015 when I was researching a book on his Cornish friend, front-row colleague and fellow farmer, the late Stack Stevens. Being a mere five years younger than John and a reasonable club standard front-row player myself, I had of course seen him play many times, both in the flesh and on television, and he always seemed to be the same. Undemonstrative, reliable and always right in the thick of things, he seldom grabbed the banner headlines but rarely, if ever, had a bad game. All the time he kept adding to a reputation: firstly for becoming arguably the most technically accomplished hooker in the entire world and, in due course, finding added fame as a highly effective leader in the most demanding situations one could ever imagine.

When I met him at the door of his attractive house, which seems to lie only a decent drop-kick away from the original Severn Bridge, he was instantly recognisable as the same man who had ruled the roost in set scrums all over the world some forty-five years earlier. His firm handshake and gentle West Country voice merely reinforced the fact that he was – and still is – very much an outdoor man of the land.

It was on the back of that book about Stevens and largely through the promptings of his son Jonathan and daughter Mandy that he was gently persuaded to, perhaps belatedly, open up about his life and rugby career. This has been written from the standpoint of rugby as it is today, looking back upon a time when the game was fanatically amateur, quaintly haphazard in terms of preparation, training and tactical appreciation but one which provided a huge opportunity for fierce competition, close comradeship and sheer joyous fun.

In Bob Dylan's early 1960s song *The Times They Are a-Changin'* he and his contemporaries reflected a major generational culture shift across not only America but indeed the entire Western world, and somehow the game of Rugby Union stood out as something of a rock against the advancing tide. That age group had never had to fight in a war nor even undertake National Service, the music of the day had passed from the American rock 'n' roll era of Elvis Presley and Chuck Berry across to the UK to the time of the Beatles and the Stones, and Harold Wilson was beginning to regale us with catchy phrases about the 'white heat of new technology'. Technology was hot but Brittannia was 'cool' and even conventional rugby players like John Pullin had begun to have long hair. Nevertheless, looking back, rugby football was still stuck in something of a time warp – cheery, occasionally violent, but for all that extremely enjoyable.

In those days there were no World Cups, European competitions nor even domestic leagues. The Rugby Union rather half-heartedly introduced a knock-out cup and in only its second year John took part in a Twickenham final for all of about forty-five seconds before being carted off with a badly damaged knee. But that was all. His club, Bristol, held a proud place in English rugby with an enviable fixture list encompassing not only the elite English clubs but those of Wales as well. They were all notionally 'friendlies' although that term was not always readily apparent on a wet Wednesday night in Ebbw Vale or Neath.

Specialist hooking as practised in the 1960s and early 1970s has unfortunately now become something of a lost art today, rather like that of punch card operators or shorthand typists from that same era and although the sport has progressed for the better on a multitude of fronts, this seems a great pity. For all that the game is much faster, the refereeing not only better but fairer, and the old free-for-alls at seemingly every line-out are thankfully a thing of the past.

In the 1960s and 1970s a high percentage of possession hooked from set scrums could often decide the outcome of an entire match. This is unlike today when packs repeatedly collapse, the ball is either tossed into the second row or fed almost at right-angles to the tunnel and so much concerted weight squeezes together that a twenty-first-century 'hooker' (my inverted commas are deliberate) often dare not strike for the ball for fear of his side being smashed backwards. This naturally begs the question as to whether a player like John Pullin could even exist in today's game.

In putting together his story I have drawn heavily upon the recollections of John himself and those of his immediate family.

I have also received generous and often enthusiastic input from a good sprinkling of his contemporaries at club, county and international levels and the deep respect and indeed affection for him was not only spontaneous but virtually unanimous.

I am therefore much indebted not only to John's own memories but also to the Pullin family in general. Furthermore, I would like to express my sincere thanks to John's twice British Lions colleague Sir Gareth Edwards for his foreword to the book.

I would also like to convey my gratitude to Mike Burton, Peter Colston, Robin Cowling, Bev Dovey, Mike Fry, Jimmy Glover, Roger Grove, Russ Hillier, Nigel Holbrook, Tony Horton, Andy Johnson, Peter Larter, David Mann, Alan Morley, Andy Munden, Derek Neate, John O'Shea, Alan Pearn, Ken Plummer, David Powell, the Pullin family (Brenda, Jeff, Phillip, Jonathan, Joanne and Mandy), Chris Ralston, Bill Redwood, David Rollitt, Austin Sheppard, Fergus Slattery, Peter Stagg, the late Mickey Steele-Bodger, Jane Stevens, Tony Swash, Bob Taylor, John Taylor, Bill Treadwell, David Watt, Tony Weaver and Peter Wheeler, all of whom have patiently answered my stream of questions.

I would also like to acknowledge the *Green 'Un, Bristol Evening Post, Radio Times* and Colorsport for the use of their photographs; Nick Grant, Kevin Paul and Jenny Stephens at Amberley Publishing; to Dave Fox and Mark Hoskins for their generous reviews and advice; and, of course, not forgetting my patient wife Micky and daughter-in-law Kath for their diligent proofreading.

To them all I repeat my sincerest thanks. All efforts have been made to identify the copyright holders of images. If any images have been used inadvertently without permission the necessary amendment will be made at the first opportunity.

Steve Tomlin
Berkhamsted, 2019

1

The Speech

John Pullin is a quiet man. Not shy or self-effacing but, as a farmer accustomed to spending many of his waking hours alone with his sheep and beef cattle, he is happy to mix as necessary but is just as content in his own company.

By the early 1970s he had risen to be almost universally recognised as the best hooker in the world, with two successful British Lions tours behind him and an automatic place in the England team at a time when selection committees chopped and changed personnel seemingly upon the merest whim. After a catastrophic season in 1972 when England had contrived to lose all four of their matches to once again finish an embarrassing bottom of the Five Nations table, the Rugby Union had finally turned to John almost in desperation to lead his country to South Africa. It seemed an almost hopeless task as no modern British team had ever succeeded in the Republic and surely this particular England team were on a hiding to nothing. Indeed, one or two of England's established players had already found an excuse not to go.

Against all the odds, England not only beat the Springboks in their own backyard but emerged unbeaten from an entire seven-match tour. When he took the job on John knew he would be required to make a number of short after-dinner speeches and actually got himself some coaching in the process. When the time came for him to rise to his feet after beating Natal in the opening game of the tour, he had remarked drily that when he told his tutor that he was the new England rugby captain he had only been taught how to deliver losing speeches so he had to suddenly come up with something new.

Outside of rugby the United Kingdom was going through what is probably still the unhappiest period in its history since the end of the Second World War. Increasingly militant trade unions were playing havoc with the economy and seemingly every football match would be blighted by riots on the terraces. The Yom Kippur War was soon to result in the OPEC countries quadrupling the price of oil in retaliation against America's support of Israel, thus causing panic in the Western economies and then there was the ongoing misery in Northern Ireland.

In February 1972 Scotland had been due to fly to Dublin to play Ireland only four weeks after the notorious Bloody Sunday tragedy in the Bogside and had decided not to travel in view of the ensuing chaos. Worse still, Wales – who were also due to visit Lansdowne Road – then did likewise and that season's Five Nations Championship thus fizzled out as a consequence.

As a wholly amateur sport, the Irish Rugby Union depended almost entirely upon receipts from home international matches and were plunged into a financial crisis. The French had generously agreed to play an extra match in Dublin to help but by the following January, with the murder and mayhem in Belfast seemingly a daily event, the question arose as to what would happen next. Anti-British feeling in Ireland was certainly not universal but it was extremely widespread and if anybody was going to represent the object of their hatred it would almost certainly be the white-shirted English.

Just before Christmas the visiting New Zealanders (who had nothing to do with the 'Troubles') had played in both Belfast against Ulster and against Ireland in Dublin under strict army security. By early February England were scheduled to play in Dublin and if they were also to pull out, the Five Nations would have been ruined for a second successive year and perhaps might never have recovered. What would the English do?

The great and the good of the RFU at Twickenham had decided that come what may they would send a team to Ireland and, in the high-handed manner of rugby officialdom at the time, did so without even consulting the players. Having taken that fateful decision, they now had to raise a team who were willing to risk their necks in England's cause.

In those days a player only learned if he had been selected or dropped by England from reading it in the stop-press column of a newspaper or perhaps hearing it on the radio. If selected, this would be followed by a postcard to his home address informing him of his selection. If he was to be omitted there would just be a deafening silence.

It was against this background and following yet another England defeat in Cardiff that John received a secret, but also unprecedented, visit from Alec Lewis and Sandy Sanders – two of the England selection committee – who called in at John's farm on the Sunday.

> They clearly wanted me to indicate that, as captain, I for one was prepared to go. They never said as much but there was the clear implication that if I didn't go they would find somebody else in which case I would almost certainly lose my England place - quite probably for ever. Perhaps selfishly I agreed there and then to go without even discussing it with my family.

Ireland's talismanic lock-forward Willie John McBride then stressed in a private phone call the importance of 'not letting the terrorists win', which is clearly how it would have been interpreted had the England team backed out. In the event twelve of the team who had gone down in Cardiff made the trip but tellingly two who declined to go – Peter Larter (then a serving officer in the RAF) and Moseley's Sam Doble – were never to be picked for England again.

In the days leading up to the match John had received one anonymous phone call advising him 'not to visit Dublin' but no threatening mail and he has since dismissed the call as possibly a hoax. For all that, it did little to lessen the growing sense of tension which of course was being magnified by the press as usual.

There were strict security precautions entailing the team training on the Friday in London rather than in Dublin and then flying over later in the day. They were met by a phalanx of Irish soldiers as well as the Garda at a separate terminal and were ushered swiftly onto a waiting bus which, with true Irish logic, had a large notice proclaiming 'ENGLAND RUGBY TEAM' emblazoned boldly across the front. It was all getting very tense as the lanky Andy Ripley, who was sitting by a window, started twitching and rocking in his seat when the bus pulled up at some traffic lights. When asked what the matter was, he replied he was just making it 'more difficult for the snipers'. It was meant as a joke but it raised some very nervous laughs. When they got inside the city centre Shelbourne Hotel they found that, in the interests of security, the Irish team would be taking the unusual step of staying in the same hotel presumably on the reasonable assumption that the IRA were unlikely to try to blow up their own team. Nevertheless, the hotel was crawling with armed police and secret agents and John and the others slept with them posted outside their bedroom doors.

One of the England wingers was one of John's teammates from Bristol named Alan Morley. He recalled how rugby could suddenly ease the general tension.

> My father had come over to watch the match with a friend and spent the previous afternoon playing golf at Portmarnock. Somebody quizzed him as to what two English blokes were doing there on a Friday afternoon but as soon as he told them he was over to watch his son play rugby against Ireland the following day it was all smiles and inevitably drinks all round.

The next day security around Lansdowne Road was everywhere and when the time came for John to lead the England team out onto the pitch, they really did not know what to expect. In Cardiff their entry onto the field had been greeted by some half-hearted clapping mingled with a few boos and the usual bit of light-hearted anti-English abuse. This time, as they emerged, blinking into the winter sunlight, they were met with an ear-splitting roar that seemed to shake their studs in the turf. True rugby fans made their feelings known – these particular fifteen Englishmen were very, very welcome.

In spite of all the precautions, the teams were still expected to line up and stand still for presentations and the Coventry centre Peter Preece recalled being reprimanded for not standing still during the anthems as he nervously scanned the roof of the grandstand for anyone who might be ready to take a potshot at him.

The match thankfully passed off without incident but England yet again came off second best and for once Ken Kennedy out-hooked John who confessed to having felt a bit uneasy whenever he had to stand still at the front of a line-out. Lock-forward Roger Uttley had made his international debut that afternoon and recalled being much more concerned about marking Willie John McBride than he was about any imaginary snipers.

John as captain was very disappointed by the team's overall display as they tumbled to a third successive defeat but the important thing was that the match was actually played and nothing untoward had occurred.

The after-match function was held back at the Shelbourne Hotel and there were probably around 200 seated for dinner. By this time, he had developed the habit of not preparing his speeches much beforehand but would just scribble down a few notes just before rising to his feet. If England had won the match he naturally would have had to have said something entirely different but, still smarting from his team's understandable but nevertheless underwhelming display, opened with the priceless line 'We may not be very good but at least we turn up', which is of course now part of rugby folklore and has been recounted a million times ever since.

It sparked a rapturous reception from all sides of the room who knew perfectly well that coming from a man as undemonstrative as John it truly came from the heart. From that day onwards the Five Nations competition has never been in serious doubt and of course has since been expanded to Six with the inclusion of Italy. Somehow in those eleven short words the quiet farmer from Gloucestershire had succeeded in capturing the very soul of rugby football.

2

Growing Up in Aust

Tucked away on the Gloucestershire bank of the River Severn is the quiet village of Aust. Most people hurtling by on the M48 would be totally unaware of its existence. Indeed, with the M5 down to Exeter also passing nearby, it forms a little rural oasis from all the concrete, steel and hubbub of modern life.

Its slightly unusual name is derived from the word Augusta and is today a settlement of some 500 souls, boasts a towered fifteenth-century church and a chapel together with the cosy Boar's Head pub and is surrounded by rich farmland. This includes Tan House Farm, which from the late 1930s was the home of Bill Pullin and his wife Eileen. This comprised roughly 120 acres with a second farm – Pear Tree Farm – just a couple of miles away. In those days there were of course no motorways to disturb a close-knit rural community but with the thriving city of Bristol with its shops and bright lights no more than 10 miles away, the couple could be said to have enjoyed the best of both worlds.

It is believed that the Pullin family came down from Yorkshire early in the nineteenth century and, following a long-forgotten feud in the family, one faction called themselves Pullin whilst the other spelled their name with the letter 'e' as Pullen. In any event, the family had all been deeply involved in farming in that part of Gloucestershire for several generations. Eileen came from a village near Cheltenham and was a qualified nurse, which must have become extremely useful when later tending to all the bumps and bruises of her three sons.

Bill had never played rugby and his participation in sport had been limited to being a reasonable club cricketer. He always had an abiding interest in horses and used to show them as well as his cattle in the local agricultural shows. He also used to like going hunting and one of John's chores when growing up was to have to ride his horse over to a local meet for his father to then take out with the hounds.

On 1 November 1941 – All Saints' Day – Eileen gave birth to their second son whom they were to christen John Vivian to accompany his elder brother Jeffrey who was by then aged two. For two years the country had been engulfed in war and by then one of their fields had a huge searchlight in it plus some Nissen huts – one way or another life had become very much harder. War had been declared only five days after Jeff's birth and by late 1940 the Luftwaffe had begun to hammer away at Bristol's Filton aircraft installations and Avonmouth Docks. Occasionally German bombers would jettison their payloads randomly on the way home. As a result, even little Aust had one house demolished by a stray incendiary and indeed one of the fields at Tan House Farm had a large bomb crater gouged out of it.

The world John came into was no longer threatened by imminent invasion but nevertheless life was still very basic. Everything was rationed, toys were either hand-me-downs, home-made or non-existent and as a result he grew up spending most of his waking hours outdoors on the farm. Tellingly his first ever memory is of picking up potatoes when he must have been no more than three years old.

He spent a great deal of his time with a German prisoner of war named Emil Jakumuit who was detailed to work on the farm and John loved nothing better than helping his new-found friend whilst Emil was relieved to be far away from the Nazis and all the horrors in Europe. Furthermore, he came from the area that was to become East Germany under the Communists and had no wish to return at the end of hostilities. He later married and settled down in England, still working for the Pullins for several more years. He was extremely good with his hands and taught his little protégé all sorts of practical skills. Pocket money had to be earned rather than doled out as if by right and John was perfectly happy sweeping out sheds, although his first attempt at hand milking was not a success – a bad-tempered cow failed to appreciate his clumsy efforts and promptly kicked both him and his bucket straight out of the door.

By modern standards West Country farms in the 1930s – and indeed up until the mid-1950s – were fairly basic places. With no mains water supply, farms usually got their water from local streams or, as in the case of Tan House, from a deep borehole. Many farms still had no electricity although the Pullins at least had the benefit of a primitive generator and large batteries which led to flickering lights and until after the war they had no telephone. An aunt nearby bought the first television set in the family and, along with homes all over the country, they all crowded around it to watch the Coronation in 1953.

There were both his elder brother and the other kids from the village to play with and together they roamed the area from dawn 'til dusk, wallowing in the mud on the side of the River Severn, climbing trees, bird-nesting, pinching apples and having impromptu football kickabouts or pick-up cricket. Whatever happened, they always got home in time for tea and nobody ever seemed to worry too much.

They did not venture into Bristol very often but were taken to the pantomime at the Hippodrome on several occasions. John's chief memory was of all the bomb damage and how easy it was to park with so few cars about and all the waste ground on the derelict bomb sites. Their father had bought the boys a small pony but neither of them really took to riding and it stayed on more or less as a family pet. Once John had been perched on a large farm horse pulling a horse rake which promptly ran away with him so, one way or another, horses were not going to feature much in his later life.

Soon after the end of the war Eileen had given birth to their third son, whom they named Phillip, and all three boys were destined to farm together. Indeed, it was this close brotherly bond that allowed the future rugby star to travel the world knowing all was well with the business at home.

When he was old enough he was sent to join his brother at a local dame school run by a Miss Trayhurn. There was absolutely no sport on offer, nor even a playground, and the food was dreadful. John has developed a reputation to this day for being a slightly 'picky' eater for which Miss Trayhurn and her revolting tinned spam has to carry much of the blame! That being said, the old girl clearly served her purpose as both boys passed easily into the local Thornbury Grammar School. In John's case he actually went a year early, which he now feels was a bit of a mixed blessing. It occupied a site which today forms the Sixth Form building of the Castle School, which itself has produced two famous rugby star alumni in Mako and Billy Vunipola.

Eileen was a devout churchgoer and the boys had to go to church twice every Sunday and sing in the choir. When John was in his teens she actually harboured a wish that he become a vicar, although he never quite shared her enthusiasm. In the days of amateur rugby this was not unheard of and one of his future Bristol and England colleagues, the late Peter Knight, actually did follow the calling. One Speech Day at Thornbury John was awarded a prize for Divinity handed to him by, of all people, Sir Stanley Rous, then the Secretary of the Football Association and later President of FIFA. On the strength of this he was promptly christened 'Holy Joe' by his buddies but fortunately that one soon died out.

Although until then John had never experienced any organised sport whatsoever, rivalry with his elder and thus stronger brother Jeff had developed a fierce competitive spirit in him coupled with an iron will never to take a backward step. The two still compete furiously to this day and even now, some seven decades later, a little game of skittles over a beer in the local pub is contested between them as if the Calcutta Cup itself was at stake. Somehow, they once got hold of some boxing gloves but their mother had to confiscate them when John's determination not to concede an inch to his elder brother had resulted in an extremely sore bloody nose. That dogged iron will to stand his ground no matter what would later serve him well throughout his rugby career, especially when standing eyeball to eyeball with a Springbok front row.

Thornbury Grammar School enjoyed a good reputation under a strict disciplinarian headmaster. One of his pet aversions was snowballs and one winter afternoon young John was unlucky enough to be about to hurl one at one of his mates at the very moment the gentleman rounded the corner and so got soundly caned as a result.

The school played football in the autumn term and rugby after Christmas with, of course, cricket in the summer. John showed himself to be a good all-round sportsman without ever being considered outstanding. He enjoyed football and began to accompany his brother to Eastville Stadium to follow Bristol Rovers where his first sporting hero was the club's once-capped centre-forward Geoff Bradford. He could do a good job as a centre half in football and was a decent off-break bowler and handy batsman at cricket who occasionally turned out for Old Down cricket club after school.

What about rugby? The sports master at Thornbury was a Mr Pedlar who had played for Clifton and it was he who gave

John his very first introduction to the basic skills of passing, tackling and kicking. His brother Jeff was already a winger but John immediately found himself placed by Mr Pedlar as a hooker. Whether this was by a flash of genius on his part or mere good luck we shall never know, but since then John can only recall ever playing in any other position when he once acted as a makeshift prop with Bristol's United XV.

The school did not have age-group-related teams and so he was in his mid-teens before he ever played in a competitive rugby match. When he finally did so it is one of those quirks of fate in that he was destined only on one single occasion to play in the school's First XV. That hooking berth was held by a little ginger lad who had the delightful name of Ernie Entwistle who has since dined out for years on the fact that he had once kept the future captain of England out of his school team. John insists that he used to out-hook Ernie repeatedly during games lessons and practice sessions but still Pedlar refused to put John up into the First XV apart from that solitary occasion against Marling School in Stroud.

He did get his first opportunity to captain a side when he led the Second XV for two matches. He took his role seriously and even kicked some of the conversions. Unfortunately, this experience came to an abrupt halt when the headmaster stripped the position off him after some busybody had reported him for smoking on the bus!

His own sports master's refusal to recognise John with a First team place merely stoked the fires of John's ambition and played into the hands of all his steely competitive instincts. If his own sports teacher would not recognise his talents others soon began to do so. A teacher at Queen Elizabeth's Hospital School, which often played Thornbury at both First and Second XV levels, spotted John's already super-fast hooking action. As a result, John found himself playing for the combined Bristol Public and Grammar Schools. This was – and still is – almost unheard of for a boy who is not already starring in his own school First XV.

Away from the rugby field, he generally did well at Thornbury and obtained the required seven 'O' Levels easily enough in the summer of 1958. However, because he had gone to Thornbury a year early and had a birthdate in November, he was forced to stay on an extra term due to some arcane rule about students having to have passed their seventeenth birthday before leaving.

He finally left at Christmas 1958 and immediately carried on working on the two farms under his father's direction although he was due to go off to Cirencester Agricultural College later in the year. At around this time he met his future wife Brenda Edwards for the first time at a local Young Farmers dance. According to Jeff he had been hoping to walk her home himself but then John stepped in and that was that.

He also decided to join a local rugby club, and so his long journey began.

3

How Times Have Changed!

The lengthy rugby career of John Pullin spanned nearly twenty years from around 1960 up until the late 1970s. Given that this is now many years distant, it may be helpful to be reminded of just what an enormous contrast exists between rugby as it was then played, administered and reported with that of today. This is not to try to gaze back through misty eyes at the supposedly 'good old days' of one's long-lost youth, but simply to give some meaningful context to his extensive rugby career.

First and foremost, it was a passionately amateur sport at every level from the famous international star right down to the portly little fellow with odd socks puffing around for the Extra B XV in front of no spectators and only twelve other men in his team. At around the time that John first emerged into the Bristol team a hilarious book came out from the late Michael Green called *The Art of Coarse Rugby* which detailed the life of the mythical Old Rottinghamians Third XV and the Bagford Vipers Extra B. What made it so funny was that so much of it was all too true.

Whilst the top teams like Bristol inevitably trained hard and looked after themselves, that culture of downing ten pints of beer after a match, playing drinking games like 'buzz', doing impromptu stripteases and singing lusty ditties about girls' knickers died hard. Indeed, for most junior clubs, takings over the bar was their main source of income and only really died out with the coming of the breathalyser.

Players were not only denied any remuneration whatsoever for playing the game (and only a very few at senior level were provided with any travelling expenses either) but players were generally obliged to fork out a match fee for the privilege of playing.

Usually this was a fairly small amount to defray the cost of getting shirts washed and chipping in for a jug or two of beer but the principle was clear: you paid for your rugby; rugby did not pay you. Furthermore, you provided your own boots, shorts and training gear and, at junior club levels, often socks and shirts as well. Kit was generally heavy, hard-wearing and the very idea of any of it bearing a sponsor's logo would have been met by a gasp of horror.

The game was also administered on a purely honorary basis by elected ex-players who saw it as a matter of pride to 'give something back to the game'. Praiseworthy though that undoubtedly was, this tended to add to the innate climate of ultra-conservatism reflecting a spirit of 'well it was good enough for me so it is good enough for them'. This theme will recur many times in the story of John Pullin.

Progressive new initiatives were generally viewed with, at best, suspicion and often outright hostility frequently based on the vague notion that it might somehow compromise the 'amateur ethos of the game', although nobody could ever clearly define what the hell that actually meant. Whilst there was a great deal to commend a major contact sport being played without any taint of money, it also led to much 'amateurishness' in matters of training, preparation, skills improvement, medical care and player safety, which, with the benefit of hindsight, seems to have been a great pity.

The Union game's administrators were totally paranoid about the sport of Rugby League which could offer a talented player a substantial signing-on fee and then modest match fees and bonuses. 'Going North' was viewed as the ultimate sin and anyone who did so was immediately cut off from all contact with the Union game and such a person was somehow considered to be a social pariah who should never again darken the doors of a Rugby Union club for the rest of his life. From today's perspective this all sounds completely bonkers – not to say illegal from the point of human rights – but that was how things then stood.

Players who could look forward to rewarding business careers rarely took much interest although a few, mainly from Wales and the north of England, sometimes rose to the bait. As a man with a well-defined farming future, John was never going to be seriously tempted.

With very few exceptions, all matches were nominally 'friendlies' in the sense that there were no formal leagues and few cup competitions. The County Championship was keenly fought and for West Country men like John Pullin it was also one of the precious few occasions when a man playing outside the elite circle of London or Midland clubs might be noticed by the national selectors.

One of John's regular teammates for both Bristol and England was Dave Rollitt who remarked how time and time again both Bristol and Gloucester would hammer clubs like Bedford, Wasps, Rosslyn Park and Richmond only to find that when the National Trials came along, it was men from those teams who were called upon to show their paces.

Without the meritocracy of a league structure, clubs arranged their own fixtures and often these continued on a reciprocal basis for decades. As a result, there were occasionally some embarrassing mismatches but, as the best players tended to be drawn inexorably to the clubs with the most attractive fixture lists, the status quo was generally maintained. Only in the early 1970s did cup knock-out competitions begin to appear both on a county and national basis in England and Wales.

Some leading clubs such as Bristol would have their games reported in the national broadsheets but it was down to just a few lines in local papers for the great majority, as was the case for John's first club, Bristol Saracens. Metropolitan clubs like Wasps, Rosslyn Park and Richmond might field a dozen or more teams on a Saturday and a player's ability to rise through the ranks was largely at the mercy of the respective team captains who exchanged impressions at a Monday night selection meeting. Most clubs ran two or three teams with standards of fitness, refereeing and playing pitches deteriorating rapidly as one descended into the lower depths of Michael Green's beloved 'Coarse Rugby'.

Some of the better junior clubs, including the Bristol Saracens, ran an Under 18 Colts team but mini-rugby only began to appear in the early 1970s. There were quite a few Veterans teams dotted around but women's rugby was still virtually unknown. Rugby club members were certainly not all unreconstructed male chauvinists but candidly quite a few still were and the fate of many wives and girlfriends, who loyally supported their menfolk, was often to be asked to butter the sandwiches, pretend to ignore the singing and help with the washing up.

Crowds, even at top-level matches, were generally numbered in hundreds rather than thousands and most clubs took far more money over the bar than they ever gleaned through the turnstiles. Bristol was one of the best-supported teams in the entire country but, even for them, a crowd of more than 3,000 to 4,000 was considered highly satisfactory. Some clubs had a grandstand and floodlights but many did not and when lights did appear, they were often only suitable for midwinter training rather than for the playing of actual matches. When Bristol and several of the Welsh clubs installed lights in the mid-1960s and wanted to form a midweek floodlit league, the RFU predictably frowned upon it and it thus became an all-Welsh affair.

Even the most cursory look at a top-level match from that period on YouTube or a DVD would illustrate a number of major differences in the way the game was played and refereed compared with today. The first thing one would notice would probably be the physical size of the players themselves. A hooker such as John standing just under 6 feet tall and weighing around 210 pounds back then might be considered a relatively big man who would be more than adequate to take the strain of an international scrum. A lock-forward at 6 feet 4 inches would be considered tall and if he weighed around 230 pounds like Bristol's 6-foot-6 Dave Watt he would be regarded as a bit of a giant. Today this is around par for many professional centre-threequarters.

Line-outs were often something of a mad scramble with players usually pushing, elbowing and barging into one another. Jumpers were not supposed to be lifted when they took off but were expected to rely upon their own natural spring to outreach their opponents. An experienced prop could usually get away with a sly 'hoik' on his jumper's shorts to gain him an extra few inches but always risked being penalised by the referee for doing so. Furthermore, the hooker was only expected to stand at the front and could leave all that tricky throwing-in stuff to the wingers.

The standard of tackling was usually significantly lower than today and all that defensive jargon like 'blitz', 'drift' and 'line-speed' were still far away into the future although good defenders already performed them naturally. Handling was far less sure than it usually is today when it is probably helped by hours of practice and the better design of modern rugby balls. There were no goal-kicking tees and a man had to create a small mound in the turf on which to place the ball, which was frequently kicked on its point in what was then known popularly as the 'torpedo' style.

The referee was the sole man in charge and even at top level he had no technology or even referees' assistants to aid him. Touch-judges were appointed by the clubs themselves and were confined to waving a flag if the ball went over the touchline and to signal successful kicks at goal. There were no yellow cards or sin-bins and any foul or unfair play was invariably dealt with by a stern 'ticking off' from the referee and a penalty kick. It was extremely rare for a man to be sent off the field and referees tended to avoid doing so if they possibly could. Scrums were far less rigidly refereed but ironically almost never collapsed. The referee insisted the ball was put in more or less straight and the rival front rows fought out their own game-within-a-game with hookers like John living up to their name by being acknowledged experts at hooking back the ball. They were perforce smaller and more flexible than their 17-stone modern counterparts but, apart from the very best ones, were not expected to contribute as much to general handling, tackling nor – as mentioned – throwing in to the line-outs.

Many people described John Pullin as being a super-fast and technically gifted hooker but at the time he was playing the skills and tactics involved were somewhat different from those employed today. Reference will be made repeatedly in this book to the 'loose-head' and the 'tight-head' propping positions. For the uninitiated, the loose-head packs onto the left shoulder of the hooker and, when his team has been awarded the scrum by the referee, the ball is put in on his side of the scrum. In the case of the loose-head, his role was to help his hooker by ensuring, as far as possible, that the tunnel was high and clear enough for the hooker to have an uninterrupted view of the ball coming in and prevent the other team from either disrupting him or pushing his team backwards off the ball. As such it was an essentially defensive skill with a vested interest in keeping things as smooth as possible.

As is still the case today with the three front men from either side packing directly against each other, the hooker would be a body width closer to the incoming ball on his own scrum-half's put-in than his opponent. This gave him a fractional advantage but precise co-ordination between the ball coming in and being instantaneously heeled back was still essential. Schoolboy scrum-halves would often call out something like 'coming in now', which of course immediately gave the game away. More experienced scrum-halves might just make a tiny movement of one of their fingers on the ball a split-second before putting the ball in. Another ploy was for the hooker to make the call himself by a subtle tap with his left hand across the broad shoulders of his loose-head prop, which obviously could not be seen by his opponent.

Conversely the tight-head, packing onto his hooker's right arm, would try to keep a straight push on his team's own put-in and then to outsmart the opposition on theirs. He might do this by either pushing the opponents off it, lowering the scrum to an uncomfortable position or boring in upon the opposing hooker and blocking his sight of the ball. This last approach was technically illegal even back then but referees only occasionally intervened. If sufficiently strong and adept enough to take all the weight on his left foot for a split second, a good tight-head would also try to sweep the ball back with his outside right foot as the opposing scrum-half put the ball in.

As a consequence, scrums played a much more important role in the game in those days with often thirty occurring in a game. Because of that a dominant hooker could make a massive contribution to the eventual outcome of a rugby match. Rather like a gunfighter in an old Western movie being quick on the draw, John, from his earliest days, had lightning-quick reactions and an abnormally fast strike with his right foot. He would particularly go for opponents' put-ins where it would make the maximum impact such as when the scrum was close to one or the other try-line. A particular ploy was to throw everything at the first couple of opposing put-ins which, if successful, could goad his direct opponent into desperately trying to get his own back and thus risk getting penalised by the referee. Another outcome was to sow doubt in the minds of the opposing team's backs who were then never quite sure whether to align themselves for launching an attack or simply moving up to shore up the defence.

As can be imagined, there were hundreds of tricks of the trade and, with minimal formal coaching, a young hooker like John would generally have to learn them from his elders or by hard and sometimes painful experience.

Most props had a strong preference for one or other position and their muscles developed accordingly. Today, packs of forwards are probably 20 per cent heavier and, with full-time professional coaching, the combined skills and weight distribution of sixteen huge men driving against one another in a closely co-ordinated shove presents a very different set of issues, including those of physical safety. The pressure generated now is so immense that a present-day 'hooker' often dare not lift his foot from the ground for fear of his team immediately being shoved off the ball and probably incurring a penalty kick. Rugby lawmakers and referees have struggled to deal with this and innumerable scrums have ended up either collapsing or resulting in the referee awarding yet another penalty to one or other team with perhaps only the sketchiest idea of what may or may not have actually happened. Such is progress.

If one looks at a modern hooker there is a fair chance he will have his socks down around his ankles, which is a sure sign that there is virtually no competition for the ball when it is tossed in at an acute angle often behind his feet. When John played he took to wearing three pairs of socks over one another and had special shin pads, made of highly reinforced plastic, inserted just to protect his shins from being kicked to pieces.

The only television station to show rugby was the BBC, who generally restricted their live coverage to international fixtures and the annual Varsity match. Almost invariably the commentary would be heard in the rich Border tones of the Hawick schoolmaster Bill McLaren, who could somehow remain irreproachably impartial even when commentating on his beloved Scotland at Murrayfield. There was never any advertising on shirts, pitches or even pitchside hoardings, which of course suited the BBC admirably.

Today pitches – at least for senior rugby – generally look immaculate and seem just as fresh and green in April as they did in September. Many of course are now partially or wholly synthetic and the rugby is greatly improved as a result. In John's day some (like those at Cardiff and Bath) would frequently flood and several international matches were battled out in a sea of slimy mud. After a few minutes the only thing spectators could make out were whites of players' eyes and teeth (if they actually still had any) as thirty men grappled with one another in what looked like a sea of oxtail soup.

Then there was always the notorious rugby tour. Clubs in the West Country and in South Wales hosted swarms of them almost non-stop during the September and April of each season. They were looked forward to eagerly by both the touring teams themselves and also by the local spectators and players who got the opportunity to watch and lock horns in action with many of the best men of the day. In time, and with the increased availability of cheaper flights, many senior clubs like Bristol began to look further afield towards places like Canada but for all that the practice still survived.

John's senior career was to take him to South Africa (four times), New Zealand (twice), Australia (twice), Zimbabwe (twice), Canada (twice), Namibia and Fiji. Those major overseas tours were unquestionably life-enhancing experiences and lasting friendships were forged between men from very different backgrounds. The rugby might have varied, the refereeing might have been infuriating, the standards of accommodation might not have been the best but they were invariably enormous fun. This held equally true whether it was a Lions tour to face the All Blacks or just a boozy college team celebrating their Easter vacation in Torquay.

There was an extra unwritten rule of rugby which you would never have found in the IRB Law Book but one which was virtually never broken. This was the mantra that 'what goes on tour stays on tour'. In other words, once players returned to their homes and families an *omerta* which would have done credit to the Sicilian mafia would descend and there matters would lie untroubled, often to the grave. There are many anecdotes to relate about quirky incidents on John's various trips abroad but in principle that unwritten law will remain unbroken. For all that most of what occurred would just be high-spirited, if sometimes embarrassing, pranks.

International rugby tours were of course much more newsworthy than a humble club excursion but the reporters who accompanied the players abroad at that time were true rugby men like John Reason, Bryn 'JBG' Thomas, Chris Lander and David Frost and not nosey newshounds. Thus, they restricted their accounts rigidly to the actual matches, training and injury reports and loyally left it at that. John's first major tour was with the 1968 British Lions to South Africa who would have cause to be grateful for that. There were also no selfies, social media, smartphones or red-top newspapers snooping around for lurid stories. Sadly, this is no longer the case as the England World Cup players in 2011 found to their cost.

When the rugby supporter in the early 1970s went along to Twickenham to watch the Pullins, Duckhams and Ripleys strutting their stuff they would have entered a cavernous old barn of a stadium which looked almost exactly as it had done in the early 1930s. There were three tall, dark double-decker stands and a huge propped bank at the south end of the ground where a spectator could still bring in as much beer as he could carry and watch a match for a couple of quid. There were precious few facilities, the toilets stank and there were no floodlights, so sometimes spectators had to spend the last twenty minutes of a match peering through the gathering gloom.

The other International venues had their own quirks. Murrayfield was open on three sides but could cram in well over 80,000 if required. Lovely old Lansdowne Road already had that railway line running under one stand and a quaint mock-Tudor clubhouse sited in one corner of the field whilst Cardiff was backed on one side by a county cricket ground and at one end by a river which had an annoying habit of overflowing its banks and flooding the pitch. Apart from Twickenham and the equally rickety old Stade Colombes all the others were in city centre locations, which added to the fun as well as the traffic.

The crowds were different as well. The mixed blessing of corporate entertaining was still some time into the future and so the Twickenham car parks were full of ruddy-cheeked 'ruggah buggahs' from the shires. These have now been largely replaced by legions of boozy bankers from the city who appear to noisily dominate the place today as they repeatedly jump up during the match to push unsteadily past people in order to go and pour yet more intoxicating liquid either into or out of their bodies.

There were as yet no tiers of replica shirts on display either. Hordes of singing Welshmen would appear in red scarves and sprouting leeks, Scots in kilts, Irish priests sporting shamrock and hidden bottles of potcheen, Frenchmen dancing around in berets with brass bands and cockerels – they were always there in abundance. Meanwhile the poor old buttoned-up English had to content themselves with an overpriced little white nylon rosette which had usually fallen to bits by half-time.

Programmes all looked the same, with the front cover a diagonal of England's white and the team colour of the opponents of the day, and would set you back 1s and sixpence, which jumped up to 10p after decimalisation. John's son Jonathan has a whole tea chest full of them.

Pre-match entertainment, insofar as it existed, was invariably provided by an immaculately turned-out military band who would lead up to the anthems by belting out a selection of sprightly tunes from West End stage shows plus a few old faithfuls like 'Men of Harlech', 'Loch Lomond' or 'Danny Boy' depending upon who was in opposition that day. As for pom-pom girls, fireworks, clouds of impenetrable smoke and laser shows? Not a chance.

International and top professional rugby today is as much a business as it is a sport. If some of this sounds unduly grumpy it is worth repeating that the standards of training, coaching, tactical appreciation, playing kit, refereeing, playing pitches, medical care, spectator amenities and media coverage together with the sheer size, pace and handling skills of the players have all progressed massively since the time John Pullin was pounding the turf in England's cause.

Whether it is all as much fun is however a moot point.

4

Early Days with Bristol Saracens

Although his rugby achievements had so far been extremely modest, John had clearly developed an affection for the game and, encouraged by his appearances for the Bristol Schools team, he joined his nearest local rugby team midway through the season in January 1959. Thornbury, which is closer to Aust, now has its own flourishing rugby club where his son Jonathan has played for many years. All that lay far into the future when John joined Bristol Saracens RFC who, based at Cribbs Causeway, were then the closest to home and it was where his elder brother Jeff had already begun to play. Very soon the principal focus of his life was to change out of all recognition.

The Saracens can trace their roots way back to 1896 when they were formed by a breakaway group from the local YMCA and were one of the original members of what became known as the Bristol Combination when it came into being in 1901. Today the club play in smart green and white hooped jerseys but around 1960 they turned out each week in rather plain myrtle green shirts.

By the time John joined them, Bristol Saracens ran four or five teams every weekend and they, together with such teams as Avonmouth Old Boys, Dings Crusaders, Bishopston, Old Redcliffians and many others were one of a host of junior clubs in the Bristol area which constituted the Combination. This was long before official leagues were sanctioned by the Rugby Union but competition among them was always fierce with plenty of bragging rights at stake every week. The Saracens also regularly ventured northwards up into the Gloucester area with fixtures against the likes of Gordon League, Longlevens and the Old Cryptians. They sometimes even crossed the water into Wales to take on the Old Boys teams from Newport and Cardiff High Schools.

Two of the biggest employers in the area were British Aircraft Corporation at Filton and the Wills tobacco business. They both ran successful teams and it was always a pleasure to play on their much superior pitches with their relatively luxurious clubhouses.

Naturally enough John started down in the depths of the Fourth XV but very quickly went up to the Thirds, which is where he finished that first season of post-school rugby. It was often said that it took five years to become a hooker and almost ten to become a good one, particularly as there was never any formal coaching and young players just had to pick things up as they went along.

At junior level there were always a lot of missed passes and dropped balls leading to a plethora of knock-ons and consequently a very large number of scrums. Because referees were far stricter with regard to the ball being put reasonably straight into the scrum, a skilled hooker like John could have a huge impact on the result of a game by not only ensuring his team enjoyed a lot of possession but – as already mentioned – just as importantly denying it to the opposition. In fact, hookers were something of a cherished breed apart who saw their role as taking part in a straight man-to-man duel with their opposite number. They all viewed their own private contests very much as a 'game within a game' and it could become something of an obsession.

In the bar after a match they would gleefully recount how they had 'won' their game 5-2 or 4-1 or whatever whilst often having only the vaguest idea of the actual score of the overall rugby match itself! It was also noticeable that they would almost never admit to having been actually beaten and after having had a bit of a nightmare they would defiantly state things were 'about even'. John lived, breathed and grew up as a tyro hooker in that almost personally competitive environment and can still recall hooking statistics from certain matches fifty years later.

Hookers were usually quite easy to spot in those days even if they had no numbers on their backs, which was then the norm outside of senior rugby. They were generally much smaller and lighter than the rest of the forwards, little wizened shrew-like creatures who could contort their bodies into all sorts of unlikely positions dangling between two generally rather tubby props in order to somehow scrape the ball back onto their side of the scrum. Others were more of the roly-poly variety and were virtually indistinguishable from their props. Typically, they were generally going bald, had very few teeth left but had rather a lot to say for themselves. Provided they won a good share of the scrums they were never expected to rush around tackling wingers or linking up in running movements and candidly often didn't go out training very much.

Into this motley crew stepped a teenage John Pullin who was already nearly 6 feet tall, well over 14 stone with a young farmer's upper-body strength, had a fine head of hair and all his own teeth, kept his mouth firmly shut and – bursting with energy – actually relished the opportunity to run around with the ball and put in plenty of tackles. Of course, he was still very much a new kid on the block with some hard and occasionally painful lessons to be learned along the way but he already had that cobra-like right foot to strike in the scrums, which was still very much the nuts and bolts of his job. He just needed to accumulate some experience as fast as he possibly could.

Throughout his life John has never been one to have a lot to say for himself, preferring his deeds on the field to speak for themselves. Even when he became captain of England, he was never one for fiery pre-match dressing room speeches. Whilst at the Saracens the teenage hooker was very quiet indeed. One of his contemporaries at the club was Nigel Holbrook who commented,

> As second team captain and a few years older I never played alongside John but of course saw him regularly around the club. Like many with farming responsibilities he would turn up, say very little, play his game, have a shower and head back home. It wasn't that he was ever unfriendly - he was just a very quiet lad.

Bill had arranged for his middle son to go to the Royal Agricultural College in Cirencester to do a one-year course in farming. By this time Jeff was studying to go into the teaching profession and John had flirted with the idea of training as a vet. At the time this then required at least an O level in Latin, which he had never studied and so that idea was never followed up.

He had acquired a van and drove himself up to Cirencester every Monday and spent the week living in 'digs' with a family in the town. He then returned to Aust every Friday in order to help on the farm, spend some time going out to a cinema or a dance with Brenda and of course playing rugby for the Saracens. The college had a rugby team which included a few South Africans and had a regular fixture with the Bristol Saracens who used to particularly look forward to a visit afterwards to 'The Tunnel', which was a popular watering hole in the town. John never actually played a match either for or against the college and tended to concentrate on studying during the week and as a result did not have a particularly active social life. In fact, his one close friend was a lad called Mac Plaice who had never played a game of rugby in his life.

Around a third of the students came from the aristocratic landowning gentry and were predestined to manage their family estates and consequently hardly ever attended lectures or did much in the way of work. John on the other hand found the course quite straightforward as he was one of the few to have already had plenty of first-hand farming experience and was awarded the McLellan medal for coming out top of his year at the end of the course.

One of the other younger hookers at the Saracens was a lad named Harvey Hill whose own father Fred had himself hooked for England in a couple of the unofficial 'Victory' Internationals played soon after the war. Fred had been something of a star turn at Bristol where he, along with his prop George Gibbs – another man honoured by England – had cleaned out many a good opposing front row despite the handicap of only having one eye. What Fred didn't know about hooking was clearly not worth knowing. Another old player who quickly recognised John's special talent was a man called Charley Jenkins who looked after the sixteen–eighteen age group Juniors. Therefore, whilst there was never any specific coaching in those days, there was a fund of knowledge within the club for an eager young player to draw upon.

It was early during that 1959/60 rugby season that he broke into the club's First XV, leap-frogging the Reserves along the way. The way this happened was one of those strokes of luck that everyone needs from time to time. The pattern at the time was that, because the club had only two pitches, the First XV and Third XV would both play either at home or away on any given Saturday with the Seconds and Fourth XV travelling in the opposite direction. Early in the season the club's established hooker had suffered an unfortunate motorbike accident just before a home fixture, by which time the Second XV had already left for their away game. In those days long before mobile phones there was no way of recalling anyone, so John was therefore catapulted into the First XV. He then proceeded to comprehensively out-hook his opposite number and the position was now his to keep.

All rugby clubs go through ups and downs and at the time the Saracens were a rapidly improving team which by 1963 went an entire season unbeaten until their very last match. However, by then John had moved on and had made his way to Bristol. The Saracens team included several players who would go on to make a name for themselves, not least a fine winger with a fearsome defence called Mike Collins who went on to star in many big matches for both Bristol and Gloucestershire and was probably not far from being an England prospect himself. Another who had made his way to the Memorial Ground only a year earlier was a highly promising back-row player named Tony Weaver.

A few years later Tony was working at Rolls-Royce, as for a time did Brenda Pullin. One day he was passing her office and popped in to say hello whilst a rather pushy young colleague was seeking to impress Brenda by telling her proudly that he was the captain of the local Whitehall Third XV. Brenda couldn't resist gently informing the lad that actually her husband was the captain of England!

With so many teams clustered around the city of Bristol the rivalry between the clubs was intense and some of the matches could occasionally get a bit wild. As a young fast hooker with his arms wrapped up around his props, John could have been singled out as an obvious target for intimidation. Fortunately, he could generally count upon the protection of a large ex-merchant seaman called Wilf Dunstan who packed down in the Saracens' second row. Wilf had fists the size of melons and a penchant for 'acquiring' souvenirs from opponents' clubhouses and was only too happy to act as a minder to his young protégé. On one famous occasion he picked up a particularly aggressive opponent who was giving John a bit of bother and tossed him into a bramble bush.

By this time John had already filled out considerably and his own physical strength gained from countless hours of farm work coupled with that steely determination was going to ensure that he could never be pushed around. He was also beginning to pick up a few of the tricks of the hooker's trade. He had learned to slip his bind slightly on the arm away from the side the ball was coming in; to read the silent signals from his scrum-half and to block the vision of his opposing hooker frequently using the considerable power he already possessed in his neck muscles.

Combination matches did not get large amounts of press coverage but one of the reporters for the *Bristol Evening Post* was a pre-war star Bristol player called Charlie 'Spud' Murphy. Apart from his reporting, Charlie was used by Bristol as an unofficial 'scout' and he would often recommend a likely young player for them to take a look at. The modern idea of an 'academy' was still decades into the future but a postcard would drop through a young hopeful's letterbox inviting him to have a game for Bristol's United XV. This was their second XV and was made up of mainly seasoned club players who would then be joined by one or two of these aspiring young 'trialists'. If they did well, they would be invited back again and studied in a bit more detail.

It was a system that worked very well in those amateur days and most of the big clubs outside of London such as Coventry, Gloucester, Northampton and Leicester as well as those in South Wales operated in more or less the same way. By and large the smaller clubs in the area were quite happy to act as feeders to the bigger fish and took great pride in seeing one of their own make it into the big time. It was also quite usual for that player as he got older to come back to his old club in his early thirties and play for a last couple of seasons passing on his experience and knowledge to the next generation of younger players.

Murphy had evidently seen enough of the Bristol Saracens' new hooker to realise he might have something a little bit special and accordingly John received that precious postcard and made his debut in a Bristol shirt for the first time when the United XV played at Chippenham. He managed to take quite a few scrums against the head, scored a try, ran around a lot, put in plenty of tackles and generally seemed to have shown up well in a 22-0 win. This was during that autumn of 1959, and, although he returned to Saracens to play out the rest of that season and the following one as well, he was invited back to Bristol United several more times so things began to look promising. In this way he continued to get these invitations to hook for the United team throughout the following season and combined this with gaining yet more valuable experience with the Saracens.

Furthermore, he was selected to play for Bristol in an end-of-season Sevens tournament, which they duly won, and the faster pace suited him well as it showed everyone that he could run and handle as well as merely hook a ball in the scrum. Once again, he had been given an early chance to shine and he had seized the opportunity.

On the strength of all this he – along with his friend Mike Collins – was invited to rejoin Tony Weaver and an ex-Saracens prop named John New and train with the Bristol club in the summer of 1961.

He was still only nineteen years old, which made him a mere baby in hooking terms, but his feet were already firmly on the lower rungs of a ladder that would someday take him all the way to he knew not where.

5

Grab Those Chances with Both Hands

John had completed his studies at Cirencester in the summer of 1961 and then returned home to work full time alongside his father on the two farms. In the sporting arena Spurs had dominated the football world to claim the elusive 'double' whilst, nearer to home, Bristol City had gone in the other direction being relegated from the Second Division, soon to be joined by Rovers a mere twelve months later. Meanwhile in the cricket world Richie Benaud's Australians had retained the Ashes with something to spare.

The previous winter the Springboks had toured the British Isles and France with a relentlessly powerful pack that had carried all before them right up to their final match against the Barbarians. John had been along to watch them just before Christmas when they crushed a Western Counties team by a runaway 42-0 scoreline running in ten unanswered tries in the process.

Pre-season training took place on Tuesday and Thursday evenings and, though rigorous and serious, for a fit young farmer constantly involved in heavy manual work outdoors it posed no major hurdle. Indeed, John often said that after farm work rugby training was almost a rest!

However, getting into the actual Bristol First team was going to be much more difficult. The incumbent hooker John Thorne had been born on New Year's Day back in 1934 and as a result was some seven and a half years the senior and moreover had already been both the Bristol and Gloucestershire hooker for six years and at twenty-seven was only now approaching his peak. He had already clocked up well over 200 games for Bristol and had appeared in an England Trial at the Memorial Ground against the redoubtable England captain Eric Evans as far back as December 1956. On top of this he had faced both the 1957 Wallabies and more recently those selfsame 1960 Springboks when he had experienced the close attention of Piet du Toit – then the most feared tight-head prop on the planet – and lived to tell the tale.

Thorne was a tough, solidly built hooker who in rugby parlance could 'look after himself' and according to a Bristol captain of the time, Derek Neate, also had one unusual attribute: 'Thorney was extraordinarily fast over short distances and in the training sprints could keep up with wingers like Mike Ellery over the first twenty-five yards.' This of course was more than enough to make a telling burst through on a rugby field. For his part, John obviously had time on his side but would in all probability need to gain plenty of experience in the United team and bide his time for a few seasons to come.

The Bristol club in the early 1960s was firmly established in the top tier of English rugby. As we have seen, all rugby at every level was completely amateur – fanatically so – and players had to supply all their own kit except for their socks and shirts, which were handed out before the match and retrieved and washed after the game. Bristol's blue and white shirts had one idiosyncrasy which it shared with Leicester, which was to have letters on their backs rather than numbers. Whereas Leicester's front row would be denoted as A, B and C (which some people rather unkindly wondered whether was as far as an average prop could recite anyway), Bristol gave the letter A to the full-back so that John as hooker spent much of his career with the letter 'I' sewn onto his back.

There were no leagues or cup competitions; fixtures were largely based upon tradition often to the extent that the same opponents would be faced at the same point in the season every year. Bristol of course had their traditional local rivals Gloucester and to a lesser extent Bath plus all the major 'First Class' English teams from the South and the Midlands. Thus, the Bristol bus would wind its way along the pre-motorway roads to Leicester, Northampton, Moseley and above all Coventry who were arguably the strongest team in the country at the time. Visits to London to face Harlequins, Wasps, Richmond and the rest were usually undertaken by train from Bristol's Temple Meads station to Paddington with the opportunity for a few beers on the journey home.

In addition, Bristol was ideally placed for regular trips across the Severn into South Wales where Cardiff, Newport, Swansea, Newbridge, etc. always provided extremely tough opposition. Finally, there were a few slightly easier matches against local 'wannabees' like Weston-super-Mare, Clifton, Cheltenham and Stroud. One other game that was eagerly anticipated was a fixture between United and a representative side drawn from all the local Combination clubs.

The club could generally rely upon a loyal supporter base of around 3,000, which went up to around 5,000 when the fervently supported Welsh clubs, Gloucester, or perhaps Coventry provided the opposition. The biggest game of the entire season was always when Cardiff came to play and this figure could then stretch up as far as 10,000 whilst County matches at the Memorial Ground would also occasionally attract around 8,000, especially if Cornwall happened to be visiting the city. Proper floodlights only made their first appearance in 1963, although some lamps were already fitted to the grandstand roof allowing for a reasonable degree of outdoor training to take place even during the middle of winter.

It was still a few years before any formal coaching was introduced into club rugby, although in Bristol's case they had the benefit of having full-back Peter Colston as their captain who in due course was to become one of the great trailblazers in the coaching field and later went on to coach the full England team for a short period. Indeed, the whole concept of coaching was rather frowned upon by many of the powers that be at the time believing it somehow smacked of 'professionalism'. Quite why that piece of tortured logic should have been allowed to hold sway for so long remains a mystery. To repeat the point John never really received any coaching worthy of the name in his life and just picked up by experience whatever he needed to complement his remarkable natural gift for striking a rugby ball in a scrum faster than anyone else.

As a result, club captains at the time, such as Colston, Neate and later David Rollitt, had a much bigger role in the selection, playing style, tactics and training of the team than is the case today. As in most clubs at the time, there was a selection committee of three comprising at the time of Percy Redwood (whose sons Bill and – briefly – Bob were to play with distinction for the club), former Welsh international Ronnie Morris and another long-serving former player named Peter Storkey. They had clearly all played the game at a high level and would take it in turns to watch the United team each week and then come up with their preferred choices depending upon availability and fitness. Selection committees were very powerful in those days but perhaps it was just a mere coincidence that Mike Collins was to marry Peter Storkey's daughter!

The fourth member of the group would be the club captain and he would generally have the final say if, on the rare occasions, there was any significant disagreement about who should be selected.

Bristol had produced a fair number of England players over the years including two famous hookers during the interwar years in Gordon Gregory and the celebrated Sam Tucker who gained no less than twenty-seven caps at a time when there were only three or four international matches in a season. The current pack which John was to now join included another famous England forward called John Currie. He was a locally born man who had started with Clifton but had made his name with Oxford University and the Harlequins from where he made up a celebrated second-row pairing in the England team with the great line-out specialist of David Marques. Together they had formed an unbroken partnership for England for over five years and their two surnames had become as intertwined in the public consciousness of rugby followers as Morecambe and Wise.

Currie had lost his place following a defeat by the Springboks the previous winter and by now Marques had largely departed the scene. However, the returning Currie was playing with all the vigour that had gained him the nickname of 'Muscles' and in this new season of 1961/62 he was to, albeit briefly, regain his England place.

In addition to the aforementioned Thorne, Neate and Currie the pack also included the quietly spoken former England prop David Hazell who had left Leicester to teach at Taunton, ex-Bristol Saracens prop John New, a young and fast-developing second-row giant in David Watt, a goal-kicking back-row man called Gordon Cripps, plus flankers (then known as wing forwards) Terry Base and Len Davies. It was a settled unit containing a great deal of experience and enough height and weight to ensure they could face up to anything any fiery Welsh packs might choose to throw at them without undue concern.

After a couple of so-called Trials (essentially run outs to see who was fully fit and in form) the season began with Thorne in his customary place in the First XV hooker's berth whilst John settled down into United to bide his time and gain some much-needed experience with hopefully the odd chance to step up as and when Thorne was called up by Gloucestershire. Fate, however, had different ideas. The team had lost its opening match to Pontypool for which Thorne was absent on the injured list but had returned to face Stroud in the midweek. However, he rated his chances of being fit to play against Newport on the Saturday as no better than 50/50 and John was therefore asked to stand by. As luck would have it, Thorne withdrew on the morning of the match. Suddenly here was a big chance. The question now was whether he could actually step up and take it.

Bryn Meredith was generally regarded at the time as the best all-purpose hooker in the British Isles and some might argue in the entire world. He had been a permanent fixture in the Wales team since 1954 and had been with the British Lions to South Africa and New Zealand and indeed was destined to return to South Africa once more the following summer. His club team was Newport, which was a side bristling with Welsh Internationals, and it was they who were next up to visit Bristol. Directly against him would be John – still several weeks short of his twentieth birthday and whose experience to date had been limited to the Bristol Combination and a tiny handful of games for Bristol United. This had to be the hardest introduction to senior rugby anyone could ever possibly imagine.

So, on Saturday 9 September 1961 he trotted out onto the Memorial Ground to make his First-Class debut. There was a big late summer crowd to welcome the teams which lined up as follows:

BRISTOL: Peter Colston, Mike Ellery, John Radford, Laurie Watts, John Coles, David Weeks, Bill Redwood, David Hazell, John Pullin, John New, David Watt, Geoff Squires, Terry Base, Derek Neate, and Len Davies.

NEWPORT: Dewi Jones, Clive Lewis, Brian Jones, Dick Uzzell, Dennis Perrott, David Watkins, Bob Prosser, Des Greenslade, Bryn Meredith, Neville Johnson, Ian Ford, Viv Jacques, Brian Cresswell, Glyn Davidge, and Algy Thomas.

The centre of attention was likely to focus upon the brilliant young Newport fly-half Dai Watkins who had made his own senior debut only the previous week against Penarth. Watkins of course was to fulfil all that early promise to enjoy a stellar career in both Union and later Rugby League. By comparison John Pullin's impending debut had rather slipped under the radar.

Nevertheless, there was a real 'Roy of the Rovers' end to the closely fought match which had been locked at six points each when Newport had to defend a scrum near their own goal line. *The Times* correspondent took up the story:

With Meredith hooking for Newport it was unfortunate for Bristol that they were without J. D. Thorne. Meredith does not often lose the strike on his own put-in but on one important occasion he did so. From a clean heel against the head scrum-half Redwood went around the blind side for a try.

The conversion was duly kicked and Bristol held on for a dramatic 11-6 victory.

The correspondent for the local Bristol *Green 'Un* was equally impressed but the new debutant was so much of an unknown that he couldn't even spell his name correctly.

Finally, after a scrummage on the Newport line Pullen(sic) hooked the ball back and Redwood was there at the heels of his back row to gather and pounce over.

Tony Reed, writing in the *Bristol Evening Post*, was equally impressed, stating:

Pullin was plunged into the fray almost at the last minute and I for one would like to add to the many congratulations he received for his senior side debut performance.

Some years later John was to recall the experience in an article he wrote for the Newport Centenary Handbook:

Looking back to that game it did teach me a great deal in a very short time as it was a case of either learning very quickly or not learning and sinking very quickly. I honestly think it is a good policy to throw a young player in at the deep end and if he is good enough he will survive.

Many modern coaches might beg to differ but, all in all, that was one hell of a start.

Thorne was going to be out for a few weeks and, following a slightly less demanding midweek match with Lydney, the next Saturday was going to be equally challenging with a visit to Swansea. They had a pack with an even more forbidding reputation than Newport. In the middle of their front row was a young bull of a hooker called Norman Gale who was universally seen as the natural successor to Meredith and indeed went on to appear many times for Wales after having moved on to Llanelli to play alongside his brother Byron.

Bristol fielded an unchanged team apart from bringing in former skipper and fly-half John Blake to line up in the centre outside Weeks. John was bursting with energy and raced around doing all those extra things a hooker was not really expected to do. On one occasion the innocence of youth led him to hurl himself onto a loose ball with the entire Swansea pack bearing down on him. Derek Neate was suitably impressed but was glad to see him get up in one piece. Lying on a ball in the path of Gale, Jim Clifford and the rest was regarded as only marginally preferable to diving onto a hand grenade.

Wales star left-wing Dewi Bebb put the 'Whites' ahead with a typical try but late in the match Bristol equalised. Once again, the press took up the story:

> Scrum-half Redwood gave out to Weeks and although the move was stemmed Bristol retained possession from the loose ruck for Davies to put Pullin over for the try.

The game finished with honours even and once again he had more than made his mark. For sure it was only from a yard or two out but in those days, hookers often went for an entire season without ever scoring a try.

On the basis that you are going to learn quickest from the toughest of assignments, the following week took the team to Kingsholm, which of course is the home of their fiercest local rivals, Gloucester. In truth most of the players from either side had been teammates for Gloucestershire on many occasions and consequently knew one another quite well. The battle was always fierce, the bragging rights were enormous but there was always a strong thread of mutual respect.

Not so among the massed ranks of customers in The Shed. Any visiting player who dropped a pass or showed the slightest hint of weakness was barracked mercilessly and the boys up from Bristol were both relatively local and regarded as big city slickers who needed to be taken down a peg or two. The atmosphere could be electric. John absolutely loved it!

This time his opposite hooker was Mike Nicholls, another typical hard-as-nails competitor and a future rival for a place in the Gloucestershire county team. Over the next decade or so they were to face up to one another on dozens of occasions and it was always a tussle which both men looked forward to. Inevitably it was quite a battle but Gloucester came out on top to the tune of 15-3. Bristol had always prided themselves on superior fitness and their ability to pinch a game in the last ten minutes, but this time it was not to be.

The Times commented,

> Young Pullin who has already gained an enviable reputation as a hooker (on this occasion with the handicap of a cut near his eye) was unable to dominate his immediate opponent Mike Nicholls.

Indeed, after just three matches, which had all taken place in the most demanding circumstances in the context of the current club scene, he had made a highly promising start.

All this prompted the writer of a local column called 'Ian Todd Talks Rugby' to put pen to paper:

> The emergence of John Pullin is the most warming news. To get the better of the Numbers 1 and 2 in Wales, Meredith and Gale, in succession speaks for itself and John Thorne will need to produce his very best to oust this promising Thornbury Grammar School boy.

Let battle commence.

6

John Thorne and the Young Contender

On the last day of September Bristol travelled to Franklin's Gardens to take on a Northampton team containing three famous but ageing England stars in scrum-half Dicky Jeeps, highly skilled centre Jeff Butterfield and the solid, squarely built prop Ron Jacobs. Bristol forced a creditable draw but it proved to be a hard lesson for John.

Looking back John recalled,

> To be honest I had a bit of a nightmare. The man opposing me was another young player on the way up called Andy Johnson. How he never got to represent England I will never know because, looking back, I think he was the fastest and cleanest striker I can ever recall playing against. He played in several Trials and was a reserve a few times but never actually got a cap. People said that he had the reputation among some referees of being a bit of a cheat and I suppose selectors feared he would get heavily penalised. Of course, we all cheated a bit wherever we could get away with it but he seemed to get picked upon sometimes.

One report of the match referred to 'Pullin's slight build', which was clearly a way of saying he had a bit more filling out to do if he was going to make it to the very top level.

With little prompting Johnson recalled that first meeting nearly sixty years before:

> John was only a kid at that time and obviously a bit of a greenhorn so it wasn't much of a contest. He clearly had

something but I had the huge advantage of Ron Jacobs beside me who was a totally immovable square object. Later we had some rare old tussles.

Indeed, the two were destined to meet many times over the next decade and Johnson was always the one who in pure hooking terms always presented John with his toughest challenge.

By this time Thorne had recovered sufficiently to reclaim his place for the next match against London Irish and so for John it was back to the United. That second string was run by an enthusiastic team secretary named Harry Nicholas but the games were often mismatches for the simple reason that many of the better local clubs like Taunton and Bridgwater (neither of which could ever conceivably have challenged Bristol's First XV on anything like equal terms) felt it somehow below their dignity to have fixtures against a second string.

This could best be illustrated by John getting a try for the United in a runaway 49-0 win at little Wiveliscombe in the northwest of Somerset. Set against his recent experiences at places like Swansea and Northampton it meant coming down with a bit of a bump. Still, these games offered a good chance to try things out, win a huge amount of ball and gain valuable experience without any undue pressure.

There was nevertheless the likelihood that, as the long-established County hooker, Thorne would soon be called up for Gloucestershire and possibly for other big matches as well. However, when the team to oppose Devon came up the selectors plumped for Mike Nicholls and as a result for John it was going to be United matches for the time being.

One of the members of the Bristol pack at the time was a Cornish second-row forward called David Mann who recalled,

> Although everyone recognised Pullin's hooking speed and general promise there is no doubt that for the time being at least Thorne was always going to be first choice. He was tougher, more aggressive and loved to come around the front of lineouts when the opposition had won the ball and rough up the opposing scrum-half.

Following a hard-fought win by United in the eagerly anticipated match with the representative Bristol Combination team he got a further opportunity. Thorne had by then won his place back for the next County game against Somerset and so another chance presented itself. Because at least half the County team was invariably comprised of Bristol players, the fixture list usually included a less demanding match on those occasions. Not only John but his friend from Saracens Tony Weaver thus found themselves included against London Hospital.

London teaching hospitals had once occupied a major role in the English rugby scene but by the early 1960s they were already losing ground to the established clubs. Guy's and St Mary's had always led the way with Kings, 'Barts', St Thomas and The London always a step behind. Indeed, London's most distinguishing feature was their almost unique blue and white checked shirts.

For this match John had the benefit of the experience of the ex-England prop David Hazell who had joined the club from Leicester when he went to teach at Taunton. As mentioned, Hazell was also a charming, softly spoken man and he and John must have constituted one of the quietest front rows around. In Tony Weaver's words, 'Apart from John occasionally asking his props to get a bit closer or further apart you never heard a peep out of them. They gobbled up all the scrums though!'

This yo-yo between the teams continued as John got further First XV matches at London Welsh and against the Metropolitan Police in a side which included all three ex-Bristol Saracens, namely Weaver, Mike Collins and John. Both matches were lost but once again the hooking honours went to Bristol.

By this time the major plaudits in terms of the overall Bristol pack were going to the thirty-year-old John Currie. Having lost his England place the previous season to the future Rugby League star Ray French, he had moved from the Harlequins to Bristol where a series of outstanding performances had resulted in him being recalled for the first England Trial at Penzance. By January he was back in the England team as Bristol's sole representative.

Gloucestershire could usually be relied upon to win the South West group but that year had failed to do so. As a result, Thorne was not to be called away for the knock-out stages in the New Year and John had to bide his time with the United – turning out against teams like Abergavenny, Llandaff and Streatham-Croydon as well as returning to Kingsholm to meet Gloucester's second team.

Games in South Wales could usually be relied upon to get a bit feisty with Welsh referees often turning a bit of a blind eye to their fellow countrymen roughing up their English visitors. It was in games such as these that John learned how to take avoiding action when a large fist came whistling up towards him in a scrum or a sharp elbow jab was aimed in his direction in a line-out. One such match against Abercarn was reported as,

> Tempers were frayed and play was held up when no less than four players were injured in a heated exchange.

Given that this was decades before players indulged in 'Hollywood' dives as they tend to do nowadays, and it was a matter of pride that – if clouted – you didn't show a chink of weakness and go down, it must have been quite a scrap. This time the local reporter was less flattering when he wrote,

> Minutes before the interval Bristol should have scored - Pullin knocking on only yards from the line.

Before the season was finished John had a few more opportunities – notably in a win at Bath's Recreation Ground. Back then Bath were not anything like the force in the land which they have subsequently become but as a local 'derby' match it was another of the eagerly awaited fixtures.

Every year there is speculation and chopping and changing over the laws of the game. There was one interesting idea – mooted widely back in 1962 – which has never seen the light of day but would have affected hookers like John deeply. This was the proposal that the ball should always be put into the scrum by the referee. Now there's a thought!

Before the season ended another young hooker named Steve Richards briefly joined the club. Little did either he or John know that before long they would be deadly rivals for the England jersey once Steve had left Oxford University, settled in London and joined Richmond.

John had every reason to be delighted by his first season in senior rugby but was well aware that it might well be some time before the selectors would ever consider him to finally succeed Thorne. Although he got a favourable mention in despatches Tony Reed, a local rugby columnist, gave the accolade for the discovery of the season to his friend Mike Collins.

That summer the Lions travelled to South Africa together with the current England hooker Stan Hodgson included as a probable back-up to Bryn Meredith. The unlucky Hodgson sustained a broken leg in the very first match against what was then still called

Rhodesia at Bulawayo to be replaced by Coventry's tough and somewhat ruthless Herbie Godwin. Amateur players returning from Lions tours often took several months to recuperate and make up for lost time at work, so there might be an opening for a new England hooker. Obviously, John was still a long way from any sort of consideration at that stage. But what about John Thorne?

Bristol started the new season with a short trip down to Devon for the Torquay Festival and took nineteen players including both hookers. It was an early experience of the fun and games of a rugby tour, although in Bristol's case it would be within very strict self-imposed limits. Although amateur, they were playing serious rugby and it was the beginning of the season that held the chance to impress the selectors, so a lot of boozing and raucous high jinks was fairly unlikely. John nevertheless thoroughly enjoyed it and got a match against the Yorkshire club Roundhay who were also on an early season trip to the South West.

He got his next proper chance of First team rugby when Thorne was selected to play for a Western Clubs team against Canada and who then proceeded to go into a rich vein of form which was soon to propel him all the way to the England team itself. The country's current occupant of the hooking berth, Stan Hodgson, was still recovering from that broken leg he had suffered on the Lions tour and there were several potential successors.

In early December Gloucestershire went down to Redruth for a South West play-off match with Cornwall and came away with a hard-earned victory in vile weather conditions during which Thorne out-hooked Redruth's Ken Abrahams (one of his potential rivals) and a few days later was selected for the second England Trial at Gloucester. He appeared in the 'Possibles' pack alongside the future Bristol props Bev Dovey and the feisty David Wrench – then with the Quins. They did well enough to gain an unlikely draw against the 'Probables' and thus gave rise to a lot of head scratching for the selectors.

That notoriously severe winter of 1963 brought much of the country and almost the entire world of outdoor sport to a virtual standstill for nearly two months. The final England Trial was accordingly postponed and then switched to Torquay and by this time Thorne was promoted to the senior England XV against what used to be termed 'The Rest'. A week later he was running out onto a freezing Cardiff Arms Park to play Wales. That particular England team proved to be the most successful for many years to come by winning three and drawing one of their four matches.

Indeed their 13-6 win that afternoon in the Welsh capital was not to be repeated for another twenty-eight years.

For John Pullin this was a clear case of bad news/good news. On the one hand there was no way the Bristol selection committee were going to prefer him to Thorne but, on the other, his constant calls away to represent both England and Gloucestershire opened the door for frequent opportunities with the club's First XV. These included two games against Cardiff and its aggressive hooker Billy Thomas, a try-scoring match with Newport after an earlier match at Sudbury against the Wasps and one of his future rivals for an England hooking shirt named Bill Treadwell.

Thus, with the spotlight on Thorne it was an opportunity for the younger man to further polish his hooking skills. A regular colleague in the Bristol pack was the giant second-row forward David Watt who had also come to the club a few seasons before with even less prior rugby experience than John – having only played soccer at school. He recalled,

> He had learned very quickly how to hook with both his left as well as his right foot and was deceptively strong. I guess working on the farm had given him very strong core muscles and he then could use his leg speed to trap a ball coming in against the head for his tight-head prop to sweep it back. He was also able to keep the rest of his body quite still while he did so and I probably have him to thank that because his hips were not sliding all over the side of my head in the scrums that I don't have cauliflower ears.

Furthermore, although he was still extremely quiet and would shoot off back to the farm soon after a match was over, he had begun to quietly tell his front-row colleagues precisely what he wanted as each scrum formed, reflecting a growing self-confidence.

By the end of April John was to have appeared in no less than twenty-two First XV matches – some six more than Thorne.

Thorne was to lose his England place following a close win against France at Twickenham to Coventry's returning Herbie Godwin but, as the season drew to a close, both of them were selected to join England's first ever official tour to New Zealand and Australia. As a prelude to the tour, the England team under the guise of 'Tom Berry's XV' (the old Leicester flanker was to manage the England party) came to Bristol to help celebrate the club's 75th anniversary and John, along with Tony Weaver, had his first experience of turning out against a bona fide International team in all but name. To John's disappointment Godwin rather than Thorne played that afternoon, so the chance for the two of them to be seen in direct opposition was passed over and for some unaccountable reason a picture of Pullin had failed to appear in the special souvenir programme prepared for the match.

Once out in New Zealand Thorne again found himself playing second fiddle to Godwin for the three Tests and only appeared once in a heavy defeat by Hawkes Bay at Napier. He nevertheless returned with a host of new experiences and a bad case of sunburn picked up in Hawaii in a stopover on the long journey home.

Thorne was still only twenty-nine and probably in his hooking prime but in those amateur days work and family commitments tended to loom larger than they do today. Having made it all the way up the ladder once would the same appetite remain?

7

Four Years to Become an Overnight Success

Season 1963/64 was an eagerly anticipated one in the British Isles not least because of the impending visit of Wilson Whineray's New Zealand All Blacks. For John it was to be a further one of gaining hard experience, bouncing in and out between the First XV and the United largely dependent upon John Thorne's availability. It was also the year that nearby Thornbury started its own local rugby team.

John began the season with a match against a star-studded Irish Wolfhounds which, as with Tom Berry's side a few months before, was virtually a full Ireland team containing Tony O'Reilly, Tom Kiernan, Willie John McBride and the rising talent that was Mike Gibson. The two brilliant Boniface brothers from France were also thrown in for good measure.

In relation to his rivalry with Thorne it was by then becoming generally accepted by everyone that in terms of striking for the ball in the set scrums Pullin almost invariably would come out on top. What had to be overcome in the mind of selectors was the obvious difference in experience and physicality which was by then narrowing month by month. As a farmer John was naturally very strong and as he filled out he soon tipped the scales at just under 14 stone 7 pounds of solid muscle.

As for experience he was to chalk up another twenty-five First team matches including a couple of games against Cardiff and a renewed head-to-head with Andy Johnson from Northampton. He also claimed tries against London Irish and Moseley at a time when a hooker scoring them was still something of a rarity.

The situation between them at mid-season was well summarised by the journalist John Mason in the local evening paper:

> For a start John Pullin, a modest unassuming young man is playing in an accomplished manner whenever necessary. Indeed, for one reason or another, he has played more games for Bristol than his international colleague. Another thing too is that Thorne, left out by Bristol on Monday and by the County on Tuesday, reacts well to the spur of competition. His best match this season I feel was for the Western Counties against the All Blacks, the very day the first warning signs of Pullin's impending succession were hoisted.
>
> The battle is not over yet by a very long way. Pullin, several years younger, will get the job full-time as it were in due course but, like any good farmer's son, is not going to count his chickens yet awhile.

Bristol were playing expansive rugby by the standards of the day. Many scrum-halves would relentlessly work the touchlines to grind their way down to near their opponents' try-line whereas Bill Redwood and the others would always be looking to develop the play wherever it was possible. In this regard Thorne was still the greater contributor.

Centre-cum-winger Jimmy Glover, who had joined the club from Oxford University, remarked, 'Although John Pullin had time on his side and won a lot of ball, in my opinion Thorne was still the better all-round player. He would pop up all over the field whereas Pullin very rarely did so.'

Thorne's match against the All Blacks took place at a packed Memorial Ground just a week before Christmas and contained no less than nine present or future Bristol players including the entire front row. The fact that they lost by only 14-22 was no mean achievement and there was the added satisfaction that one of the Western Counties try-scorers was Mike Collins.

By this time John's father Bill began to come along to quite a lot of the home matches, especially the frequent midweek ones when it would not clash with his first love of point-to-point racing. He began to enjoy the interest and banter from his farming friends about his middle son's growing rugby reputation whenever he went to local livestock markets and as time went on he became quite a well-known face around the Bristol club.

David Watt recalled that he once visited the Pullin farm and was greeted by Bill and the two sat down in the kitchen with a bottle of Scotch. 'I learned far more about John from his Dad than I ever got from the man himself despite playing with him for years and us both touring Canada and South Africa.'

After a busy summer on the farm it was back to Bristol but for a while – apart from being in the first pick for a local 'Cavalcade of Sports' Sevens tournament – his rugby was almost entirely confined to the United XV with its predictable succession of easy victories against relatively minor West Country clubs. In one runaway win down at Sidmouth it was reported that 'in the set scrums Pullin reigned supreme'. That was all very well but, with due respect to clubs like Sidmouth, it was starting to become frustrating playing at that level when, for all his undoubted modesty, he honestly knew deep down that he was by then becoming the best hooker in the club.

The Bristol United front row had been joined by the cheery Tony Rogers and a budding psychiatrist with a massive frame and the eye-watering name of Jan Szyskiewicz (his teammates just called him 'Satch') but the most intriguing newcomer to be included in the United team to visit the Welsh village of Crumlin was Richard Sharp. The blond former England fly-half, the darling of Twickenham and Fleet Street for a brief period in the early 1960s, was still only twenty-six years old and had just begun a teaching appointment at Sherborne.

The event attracted a considerable flutter in the media although, true to form, the dear old BBC blithely announced that Crumlin would be playing against the 'United States'. Sharp continued to make the newspaper headlines and – on his day – was still a sight to behold running with the ball although his well-documented defensive frailties and his obvious distaste for getting caught with the ball and roughed up by beefy Welsh forwards did not really impress the Pullins and Rollitts of this world.

John got a couple of run outs in the First team against the Saracens and Clifton but that was all until early December when, following a string of indifferent results, Bristol fans saw their team take a bad hammering by Newport on their own home ground, at which point the selectors finally saw fit to wield the axe. Under the headline 'Withering Fire from Selectors', it was announced in the evening news that, 'A third of the team previously regarded as the best available found United team cards dropping through their letter boxes. These included Derek Neate, David Weeks and John Thorne.'

From this point onwards, it was always going to be the young farmer from Aust who would be the first choice – a situation which, despite long periods away representing his country and travelling the world, would continue for the next fourteen years.

It was perhaps unfortunate that his final elevation came too late in the season for any higher honours to be considered, especially as he had yet to put in an appearance for Gloucestershire. The England hooking berth was hotly contested that year but was eventually claimed by Steve Richards, the young Oxford Blue who had briefly played for Bristol and was now plying his trade for Richmond. The two met in February with honours probably shared evenly but John now had the opportunity to perform on a regular basis against all the other contenders on the first-class circuit. These included names like Pat Orr (Harlequins), Don Lane (Moseley), Peter Edwards (Leicester) and Bill Treadwell (Wasps), plus his old adversaries in Herbie Godwin, Mike Nicholls and Andy Johnson, not to mention the likes of Norman Gale, Vic Perrins, Billy Thomas and John Isaacs over in Wales.

To date he had missed very few games due to injury although he had picked up his full share of cuts, bumps and bruises as was only to be expected. A stomach bug ruled him out of a match with Rosslyn Park which gave a first chance to his old Bristol Saracens mate Harvey Hill who had recently followed the yellow brick road up to Bristol and would later deputise for John on quite a few occasions.

Overall it had not been a vintage season for the club by any stretch of the imagination. Wins over Swansea and Leicester and lesser lights like Esher and St Luke's College did not really make up for going down to Gloucester at Kingsholm and Cardiff when John had to battle hard to counteract the boring in from his future Lions colleague John O'Shea. Furthermore, an exciting game was lost at home to the Harlequins despite a thrilling 70-yard try from Mike Collins.

In August of that summer John got married to Brenda at the church in her home village of Olveston and Mike was one of the guests. Like a true rugby man, he had ensured that it didn't interfere with the rugby season. Due to some none-too-clever diary co-ordination his other great rugby pal from his Bristol Saracens days Tony Weaver missed the wedding as he had himself got married only the previous Saturday and was still away on honeymoon. For their part John and Brenda took theirs over in Jersey and she still insists that he has never taken her away on such a good holiday since.

The newly-weds settled into a lovely cottage just outside Aust and John returned to claim his rightful place in the Bristol pack.

This turned out to be John Thorne's last season with the club he had served so well and, having the right build for the job, became a temporary prop forward alongside his colleague in several matches.

That autumn of 1965 was when it all started to happen in something of a rush. In late October John made his County Championship debut for Gloucestershire against Somerset by the seaside at Weston-super-Mare to be followed by a much more taxing match down in industrial Camborne against Cornwall. Back in the 1960s the County Championship really meant something and it was always watched closely by the England selectors. In Cornwall it was something of a local passion and there were nearly 10,000 in the packed Recreation Ground to watch the two great rivals slug it out on a typical cold and blustery Cornish afternoon.

It was never going to be a spectacular match and it consisted mainly of the Gloucestershire pack dominating the scrums for Gloucester's bouncy scrum-half Mickey Booth to work the touchline down to near the Cornish try-line only for Cornwall's England full-back Roger Hosen to send them all the way back again with his siege-gun right boot. Gloucestershire squeaked the match with the only score being a single penalty from the then current holder of the England full-back position Don Rutherford.

John's props were his recent Bristol colleague Bev Dovey and Gloucester's Bob Fowke who were up against Cornwall's redoubtable coalman Bonzo Johns and Will Carling's father Bill who was in the army at the time and had somewhat surprisingly ousted one of John's great future England comrades-in-arms Stack Stevens who was merely looking on glumly from the grandstand. It was also the first time John faced Cornwall's own fast-striking young hooker Roger Harris – another man whose path was to cross with John's many times in the future.

If it had been a match of few frills and little to entertain the crowd it was one which caused the name 'J. V. Pullin' to become one of great interest to the England selectors. The previous year's hooker, Steve Richards, was out of contention for the time being with an injury and so the position was there for someone to claim. The question was, who was it to be?

The next county match was, if anything, an even more turgid affair than the last as a grim 0-0 draw against Devon was battled out in the mud at Kingsholm. It did however allow John to again do well against one of his other potential hooking rivals in the Devonport-based young naval officer Terry Scott who had impressed enough to have already represented the Barbarians.

After all the toil over the past four seasons and his yo-yo selection saga with Thorne, John had at last progressed from being just another face around the senior rugby circuit to being seen as a potential 'name' in the immediate future. All of this had only happened after firstly dislodging a current England hooker at his own club and – perhaps belatedly – getting recognition by Gloucestershire.

The door was now slightly ajar. Could he somehow force it open?

8

Just Another One-cap Wonder?

For the past thirty years or so – and certainly since the sport of rugby turned professional – all national rugby teams have developed a squad system. This entails around forty of the available top performers being brought together regularly for intensive coaching and conditioning work under the microscope of a group of highly professional specialist analysts and coaches. In all probability they will have arrived there through an established elite pathway involving international recognition at schoolboy, Under 20 and A-team levels as they are groomed to compete at the highest level of the sport.

Furthermore, by playing professionally, often in front of 20–30,000 plus crowds, and taking part regularly in European club competitions, a young man stepping out for his international debut will receive far less of a culture shock than had been the case back in the mid-1960s.

Schools then placed more emphasis upon team games than is generally the rule today and sports teachers were there to teach the rudiments of the game, but generally that was as far as it went. Some schools in both the state and fee-paying public schools had the luxury of employing a current or past top rugby player and a few of them had the necessary coaching skills to take some of the rough edges off a promising young player but that was just a matter of chance. Most had to teach several sports other than rugby and they often had to teach another classroom subject as well, so only a precious few had the time or indeed the motivation to impart much beyond the basics. When we add in the fact that coaching was conspicuous by its absence in adult rugby as well the development of the younger talented player it was an extremely hit-and-miss business.

Mention has already been made of the selection committee at Bristol but this system was mirrored at County level and also when it came to picking the England or indeed any other international team. In the middle of the 1960s these were all ex-international players of some note who clearly knew and loved the game but were inevitably seeing everything through the prism of their own past careers. A good balanced committee would include experienced representation of all the different positions on the pitch but matters usually came down to a majority vote for each of the fifteen selected players plus a couple of travelling reserves. These unlucky souls might be able to step in if a player was taken ill or injured himself before the match but could never be used to replace an injured man once the game was underway.

The favoured system was to have a series of public 'Trial' matches between thirty of the in-form players whom the various selectors had decided they wished to watch in a live match in opposition to one another. In England's case there were usually three of these with the first two played on a provincial club ground with the final one taking place at Twickenham in early January.

The first would often see the teams fairly jumbled up after which those who were seen to have shown up the best became the putative senior team – usually known as the 'Probables' with those who had not quite made the cut but had done well enough to be watched again known as the 'Possibles'. Finally, an 'England XV' would appear at Twickenham pitted against what was clearly seen as the understudies and rather disparagingly referred to as 'The Rest'. It was then not at all unusual for those picked for 'The Rest' to get sufficiently wound up to go out there and give the 'England XV' a bit of a going over, win the match and thereby chuck a massive spanner in the entire works.

Most people even then agreed it was a highly flawed process but nobody seemed to be able to come up with a better alternative. A hooker like John was massively dependent upon the ability of not only his props, but the shove he was getting from the back five in the scrum and the degree of co-ordination he might achieve with a scrum-half whom he had possibly never even met before. Similarly, a winger might be a wonderful prospect but never get a pass all afternoon and get lost without trace. A prime example of that would have been Coventry's Peter Jackson who suffered precisely that fate in 1950 and disappeared from International recognition for a full six years before he re-emerged as a scoring sensation and to be widely recognised as one of the very best right-wingers in the game.

The selectors at the time were chaired by an ex-back-row forward named Brian Vaughan who had been a senior officer in the RAF and had managed the British Lions in South Africa three years before. The other members comprised Albert Agar who was an ex-Harlequins and England centre, former England fly-half Ricky Bartlett and Micky Steele-Bodger, another ex-England flanker and a leading light with the Barbarians. Finally, there was Eric Evans from Sale who had captained England to their last Grand Slam back in 1957 and had amassed twenty-nine caps for England as a hooker with one more as a prop. He was clearly going to be the man who would need to be suitably impressed if John was going to be successful.

John received his card for his first trial the day after the Devon match and found it was to take place miles away at Gosforth, which is situated on the northern side of Newcastle and as such is closer to Murrayfield than it is to Twickenham. Running through the selected sides he saw that he was in what appeared to be the more senior team on paper and that he had two experienced props beside him. One of them was Coventry's iron man Phil Judd, who was the cornerstone of what was then indisputably the best club pack in England. The other was a younger man called Tony 'Pinky' Horton whom John unhesitatingly nominates as the best tight-head he ever packed down beside.

Being a farmer, John had developed a very strong neck on his shoulders but Tony Horton's was massive. He reputedly had a collar size of 21 inches, a barrel chest and an immensely powerful torso all supported by surprisingly short legs. This allowed him to be perfectly comfortable taking his opposite prop much lower than the man would have wished and then to generate tremendous power from a low centre of gravity. His immense neck produced all sorts of problems when it came to buying shirts, so he had his made especially for him out in Hong Kong and these were invariably smart monogrammed affairs in a fetching shade of pink, thereby giving rise to his nickname.

On top of all this he had a very nimble right foot which could sweep back an opposition put-in to the scrum almost at will. He had played throughout the previous England campaign and was by then something of a hooker's dream. He would frequently just ask John during a match what height he wanted the scrum to be and promptly lock his opposite number exactly as requested and they could then use their combined almost inhumanly strong necks to angle in on their opposing hooker and the strikes against the head then followed in a steady stream.

John travelled on the train all the way to Newcastle along with his club mates David Watt and David Rollitt. They had been allowed to claim for a first-class train fare but already knew the ropes enough to buy second-class tickets and pocket the difference. Don Rutherford got on the train at Gloucester and apparently went the whole way in the guard's van. Whether he ever had a ticket of any description we shall never know.

Northumberland in December was predictably arctic and what the selectors deduced from it all would be hard to fathom. The game finished a low-scoring draw, although nobody cared very much, but, with Horton at his side, John comfortably got the ascendancy over the promising Loughborough student John Elliott who later went on to play many fine matches for Leicester until the advent of Peter Wheeler.

Propping alongside Elliott was another young, and until then virtually unknown, farmer called David 'Piggy' Powell – a common nickname for farming rugby players which also followed John around for many years although he has always hated it. Powell was a powerful apple-cheeked lad with a thick mop of blond curly hair and two cauliflower ears who apparently supplemented his training at Northampton by running across ploughed fields with a bag of corn on his back. The press loved that sort of thing.

John was told to change sides at half-time but continued to do well with his new props and thus came away having created a favourable impression. Most of the headlines however went to a slight, rather bohemian scrum-half who had suddenly emerged from seemingly nowhere at the Harlequins called Jeremy Spencer. He was extremely quick and had a good length of pass but what the media loved was that he was a budding artist, weaved many of his own clothes and apparently lived in an old bus. Sadly, professional rugby fails to produce characters like that these days.

Spencer had been lucky enough to have been paired with the veteran Phil Horrocks-Taylor who was based in the North East and thus knew the conditions well and as a result shone out like a beacon through the icy gloom.

Two weeks later a second Trial took place at the exact opposite end of the country down at Torquay. That elegant watering hole for retired colonels and dear old ladies escapes the Gosforth chill but leading up to Christmas gets plenty of rain. The pitch was a total mudbath and how any set of selectors could glean much from a match played on that was hard to fathom. John was in prime position in the 'Probables', again alongside Judd, but now with his new farmer friend Powell at loose head whilst Horton was inexplicably relegated to the Possibles. This time his hooking opponent was Don Lane from Moseley and again John emerged with a 7-3 tight-head advantage mostly gained in the second half.

The final Trial was held in the vast cavernous emptiness of Twickenham on New Year's Day and having held his place to perform in the England XV, he was only too aware that he was only one decent match away from becoming an International and henceforth having one of those little asterisks after his name on match-day programmes for the rest of his life. Despite having many wonderful memories and a lot of success at Twickenham, John confesses to never having liked the place very much. 'A bit of a mausoleum' was his description of the old pre-war stadium with its three towering Archibald Leitch double-decker stands which were for many years painted in a mournful brown colour and later in an only slightly improved dark green.

Be that as it may, the selectors had lined up a third different hooker to oppose him and had settled upon Bill Treadwell from the Wasps and a man John had met a few times already. True to form, the 'England XV' captained by the previous season's England flanker Nick Silk were narrowly beaten by 'The Rest' after which there was a lot of head scratching to be done before the team was announced. For all that, with Horton back by his side, John was again well ahead on the scrum count when the game was over and by then felt quietly confident.

After the match John recalls standing up by the bar when the Chairman of Selectors, Brian Vaughan, approached him from behind and wrapping an arm around John hugged him closely rather like a large grizzly bear. 'How does *that* feel Pullin?' he asked loudly. Slightly taken aback and by now not too sure what being picked for England might possibly entail, John simply gulped and said nothing. 'That's what a prop should feel like son – you haven't been bound on to one all afternoon!' roared Vaughan. They all had clearly tumbled to John's arm-slipping tactics but seemed more amused than perturbed by it.

John cannot recall exactly how he knew he had finally made it into the team but the next morning the official letter telling him he was selected dropped into his letterbox. It was of course a big piece of news around Thornbury and Aust and the local papers gave it plenty of coverage.

Players were all issued with two stand tickets, which went to Brenda and his father Bill, and there was a whole screed about what one should wear with much emphasis on a dinner jacket, the claiming of legitimate expenses, what kit to bring but precisely nothing about the rugby itself. The match was to be the traditional opener of what was then the Five Nations against Wales at Twickenham and was bound to be a 70,000 sell-out as thousands of red-scarfed and leek-toting Taffies made their biennial pilgrimage from the valleys to the fleshpots of London.

They would have travelled with a lot of confidence too. The previous year they had won the Triple Crown and had defeated England in Cardiff with a bit more to spare than the 14-3 score might indicate. They had retained eleven of that side although they had ditched their controversial touchline-addicted captain Clive Rowlands for the more expansive Allan Lewis and had unaccountably left out their star winger Dewi Bebb.

Poor old Nick Silk had been unceremoniously dumped for ever by the selectors after the Twickenham Trial and the team were to be led by the experienced Budge Rogers. However, apart from John, the team included no less than five other new 'caps', none of whom would have ever experienced a crowd or an atmosphere remotely akin to what they would now have to face. It was just going to be a case of sink or swim.

In those passionately amateur days the team only met up on the Thursday evening and were housed in a weird hotel which John describes as being like an old people's home. Wizened elderly ladies in carpet slippers would emerge noiselessly from behind dark wooden doors and creep around the corridors to the extent that the players felt obliged to converse in a whisper.

His fellow debutant David Powell remembers it well:

> They used to have their sherry and one or two other drinks locked away in a cupboard and whenever they poured one out they would carefully mark the bottle with a pencil. I soon got fed up with this so Phil Judd and I went down to the local pub and each had three pints of Guinness. I slept like a baby but my room-mate Keith Savage who hadn't touched a drop was up and down all-night fretting about the match.

The following day Rogers had them out doing a bit of training and worked out the basics like line-out signals, who took the kicks etc., but that was about the size of it – then it was back to that old folks' home.

Come the big day Bill and Brenda joined the packed throng bringing those cavernous old stands into vibrant life. Behind one goal on the enormous propped bank stood thousands of noisy singing Welshmen; the usual leeks were hung on crossbars and their carriers cheerily chased away by London bobbies and so the stage was duly set.

The teams lined up as follows:

ENGLAND: Don Rutherford, Ted Rudd, Terry Arthur, David Rosser, Keith Savage, Tom Brophy, Jeremy Spencer, David Powell, John Pullin, Phil Judd, Mike Davis, Colin Payne, Bob Taylor, David Perry, and Budge Rogers (capt.).

WALES: Terry Price, Stuart Watkins, Ken Jones, Keith Bradshaw, Lyn Davies, Dai Watkins, Allan Lewis, John Lloyd, Norman Gale, Denzil Williams, Brian Price, Brian Thomas, Gary Prothero, Alun Pask (capt.) and Haydn Morgan.

From John's point of view the match seemed to fly by and was over almost before he knew it. He was angered by the fact that one of the Welsh lock-forwards gouged him in the eye quite early on but did quite well against his old adversary Norman Gale. Each team scored a try but Wales won by 11-6 thanks to two penalty goals from their youthful Llanelli full-back Terry Price. Unfortunately, the normally reliable goal-kicker Don Rutherford couldn't hit a barn door that afternoon, missing six kickable shots at goal, and the match was a lost cause.

That evening the RFU committee and their wives were staying up at the London Hilton where the official post-match dinner and dance was to be held. The Rugby Union bigwigs were certainly never going to take their wives to that 'old folks' home' hotel – perhaps by then some of them might have got mistaken for inmates! By contrast players' wives like Brenda were invited to the dance but oddly not to stay for the night, so John had to forsake his lovely young bride to share a room with Don Rutherford. Welcome to the big time.

An agonising three weeks were to pass before the next team to face Ireland was to be announced. Selectors had a nasty habit of wielding the axe after a defeat as though all their earlier hard work was somehow an irrelevance, so there were bound to be some casualties. It was just a question of who and where.

Sure enough, early in February the news came through. Out went the darling of the moment Jeremy Spencer to soon disappear from the senior rugby scene almost without trace, centre David Rosser, the ever-dependable Mike Davis, flanker Bob Taylor and, to his profound disappointment, John himself. Bill Treadwell was given the hooker's berth and was to hold it for the rest of the season.

John was bitterly disappointed and had visions of never getting another chance. His brothers teased him gently about being a 'one-cap wonder', which he only endured through gritted teeth. When challenged with the notion that 99 per cent of rugby players would give almost anything to get just one cap, he felt that having just a single appearance to his name smacked of failure and all his old competitive instincts flooded through him anew.

One-cap wonder – like hell!

9

Getting Back Isn't So Easy

The summer of 1966 will always be remembered in England as the summer of Bobby Moore, Nobby Stiles and everything to do with the World Cup. Like the rest of the country John was glued to the television watching our footballers' brief moment of triumph. At the same time – and in some ways almost forgotten – the British Lions had gone out to Australia and New Zealand and had suffered a humiliating 0-4 whitewash at the hands of the rampant All Blacks.

Following John's single cap against Wales, England, with Treadwell as the new hooker, had scraped a draw with the Irish but then went down to both France in Paris and Scotland at Murrayfield to finish bottom of the table and to take the dreaded mythical 'wooden spoon'. Not surprisingly very few Englishmen made it into the Lions' squad and those that did were somewhat surprising.

One of these was Piggy Powell who had himself been dropped after receiving a torrid time from Ireland's Ray McLoughlin in his second match. He recalled, 'Nothing against Bill but he was nowhere near Pullin's level and Ken Kennedy was much too quick and strong for him.'

Powell was then omitted in favour of Tony Horton but soon – perhaps surprisingly – found himself selected for the British Lions. In fact, he was the only England forward to go to New Zealand but never got into the Test team which was repeatedly outgunned by the All Blacks.

For his part John had gone back to Bristol for the rest of the season determined to keep himself in the eyes of the selectors. At Easter he received a pleasant boost to his morale when he was invited to play for the Barbarians on their annual tour of South

Wales. It was a much-sought-after accolade which until a few years ago was considered to be an honour almost on a par with being awarded an International cap.

The 'Baa-Baas' were run by a small committee of elderly rugby devotees including its long-term President Hughie Glyn Hughes, a much-decorated Brigadier Surgeon who had served in both world wars. He was accompanied by two elderly but dedicated Scots in Jock Wemyss, who had played with distinction for his country despite losing an eye in the First World War, and Herbert Waddell, who had been a distinguished fly-half for both Scotland and the Lions in the 1920s and whose son Gordon was later to emulate him.

Of a rather younger vintage, they also included Micky Steele-Bodger and Vic Roberts who had at one time vied with one another just after the War for England recognition as what had then been known as 'wing-forwards'.

Together the Barbarians had developed a great spirit of fun coupled with high standards of rugby with a pronounced accent upon running with the ball and scoring lots of spectacular tries. Although the rugby was taken seriously the result was generally felt to be secondary to putting on a good show and giving the big Easter crowds – which invariably turned out to see them – plenty to cheer.

They would only invite leading players who they felt showed the right spirit towards playing the game and could be relied on to behave themselves on and off the field. It was not especially snobby in that coal miners, factory workers and trawlermen were just as welcome as the 'Varsity' types. In other words, a quietly spoken Gloucestershire farmer would fit in perfectly happily and have a very enjoyable few days with some high action rugby thrown in for good measure.

They always stayed at the old Esplanade Hotel in Penarth which was a quaint old Victorian seaside building which has since now sadly succumbed to the bulldozers. It was a very relaxed atmosphere. There was no signing into a register and players were free to help themselves to midnight feasts from the kitchens, dress up in drag, form impromptu brass bands and play hide and seek in the cupboards – but there were certain limits old chap! One well-known Cardiff forward who had craved the chance to be a Barbarian reputedly got carried away the night before his first game and was seen to relieve himself into the fireplace. That was decidedly not within the Barbarian code and he never got to play for them.

The Esplanade would be their base for the next five days with a match each day except Sunday which was set aside for compulsory golf. John had played it a little bit in the past but handicaps never mattered as the competition was always divided into small teams, each of which would contain a couple of keen golfers, some very 'occasionals' such as John and one or two who had never picked up a club before in their life. It was all great fun.

When asked what he particularly recalled about John, the now ninety-two-year-old Steele-Bodger remarked drily, 'Excellent chap, excellent captain, excellent player but a bloody awful golfer.'

John disputes this emphatically and states categorically that he walked away with two if not three golf trophies from those tours!

As usual there was always going to be a lot of singing and party games; on the first night every new member was obliged to do a small variety turn – usually singing a song, performing a tap dance, playing an instrument, reciting a monologue or something similar. John was down to sing a duet with the All Black full-back Mike Williment who promptly ratted on him shamelessly and retired to bed with a migraine leaving John to sing all on his own. He somehow got by.

He was selected for the traditional Good Friday first match against the local Penarth club in a strong side led by the former England full-back John Willcox and played his part in a routine 12-8 win. This match brought him to play beside the as yet uncapped Scottish prop Sandy Carmichael with whom he would in due course share many ups and downs as their careers progressed.

The big matches were on the Saturday against Cardiff and the Easter Monday fixture at Swansea with a final one at Newport when players' minds were probably turning to the journey home and then getting up with a sore head to go back to work. John missed out on the big Cardiff fixture but played his second match in a thoroughly entertaining win at Swansea when he had his favourite prop – Tony Horton – back beside him to plunder plenty of ball and to bring about a convincing win. He was to have many more exciting times with that famous and wonderfully eccentric old touring club.

Returning to Bristol for the new season, John discovered that Thorne (who by then had reached the age of thirty-two) had already left the club and joined nearby Cleve, which was one of the local Combination clubs. He was of course now a regular in the team which struck a particularly good run of form that autumn winning virtually all their matches apart from going down twice to Cardiff. Gloucestershire on the other hand had a relatively thin time of it losing out to both Cornwall and Somerset and thus failing to even qualify for the latter stages of the County Championship.

In early October England staged an early Trial at Brighton where John had the satisfaction of completely dominating the scrums and in doing so totally slaughtering one of his hardest opponents Herbie Godwin into the bargain. Meanwhile Bill Treadwell had stepped down from senior rugby to concentrate on his new dental practice. John thus remained in the 'Probables' for both of the following Trials and all seemed set fair when the curse of that England XV versus The Rest fixture was to strike again. The Rest XV, with hooker Steve Richards now restored to form and fitness, duly demolished the selectors' first choices by four tries to nil and everything was back up in the air. When the invitations went out John was named only as a Travelling Reserve as Richards had seemingly done just enough to regain his place.

In those days it will be recalled there were still no replacements allowed once a match had been kicked off so the lot of the Travelling Reserve was not a happy one. He was condemned just to sit in the stands probably secretly hoping that the man in possession might get (mildly) injured so he might get in for the following match.

The local team Thornbury had only begun life a couple of years previously but they had now completed their changing rooms at their Coopers Farm Ground. To mark the occasion a team largely consisting of Bristol regulars was raised with the rather grandiose title of 'John Pullin's International & County XV'. In those rather more carefree days of amateur rugby it was very much the usual practice for pick-up teams of former and current star players to come together to support all manner of junior club events, fundraising for local charities or simply to mark some sort of jubilee celebration. These often took place on a Sunday or at the tail end of a season and although never too serious gave a great fillip to the club in question.

That season there were to be five England matches as the Australian Wallabies were undertaking a British tour. In truth they were nothing like as powerful as either New Zealand or South Africa and those Lions, who had endured such a torrid time in New Zealand, had recently thrashed them in a one-sided Test in Brisbane. They had started with a well-established hooker in Peter Johnson but quickly lost their back-up one, Ross Cullen, when he was sent home in disgrace for chewing a sizeable chunk off the earlobe of an opposing Oxford University prop.

The Aussies' halves Catchpole and Hawthorne did particularly well when they came to Twickenham for the first International and over-ran a frankly disjointed looking England. Having lost quite heavily, wholesale further changes were made although John was destined to spend that entire season's Five Nations watching Steve Richards perform from a seat in the stands. For two of his Bristol mates it was a happier outcome as both Watt and Rollitt played in all four of the remaining matches.

He did get his chance when the Wallabies came to Bristol in mid-January to oppose the Western Counties (which included his friend Mike Collins) and was able to play a full part in a rare 9-0 win for the combined side. He was also able to pit himself directly against Peter Johnson and did enough to remind any selectors present that he was still there, willing and perfectly able.

For the rest of the season Bristol lost a little of the consistency they had shown in the Autumn but still contrived to win the majority of their matches with John only missing a few due to his watching duties at the Internationals when his place was usually covered by his old Bristol Saracens colleague Harvey Hill.

He had clearly made a good impression on his Barbarians debut the previous Easter because he was immediately invited back for a second one and this time took the field against the other two traditional opponents – Cardiff and Newport. The Cardiff game was always played on the Saturday and, despite Easter falling a week before the end of March, it drew the usual huge crowd to the old Arms Park only a year before it began to be demolished and rebuilt.

Although the Cardiff game was lost by a narrow margin, John, with Powell and his favourite Tony Horton alongside, took plenty of ball in the final match at Newport to pave the way to a solid victory. He was beginning to really enjoy the general approach of the Barbarians, so much so that he agreed to serve for a while as a Barbarian committee man after he had retired from playing despite his general aversion to meetings and the administrative aspects of rugby.

But for now, he just wanted to get his England place back.

10

An England Fixture at Last

In some ways 1966/67 had been a good season for John but nevertheless it was a time when he had been forced to sit and watch a moderately successful England team from the sidelines. His club colleagues David Watt and David Rollitt however had played in all four of the Home Internationals but they would have much preferred to have John making up a trio. Rollitt remarked, 'There was no question that John was a much stronger player and a far quicker hooker than Steve Richards but the selectors at the time still seemed to show a distinct bias towards London and Midland clubs.'

That autumn of 1967 the All Blacks were to make a truncated tour of Britain and France and Rollitt's words of criticism were to be vindicated totally by the team which eventually was selected for the big match in early November when they were comprehensively beaten at Twickenham by the New Zealanders.

To the outside observer, the behaviour of the selectors was baffling to say the least. After a slightly better season in 1966/67, during which victories had been gained over Ireland and Scotland coupled with a narrow loss to France, England had been outplayed at Cardiff in mid-April in a thrilling match that went down in history as 'Keith Jarrett's Match' when the eighteen-year-old debutant racked up no less than nineteen points – which included a thrilling individual try – in a crushing 34-21 victory.

The England selectors had correctly retained virtually all of that squad for a flag-waving short tour of Canada prior to the All Blacks' arrival. They had replaced the ageing Roger Hosen at full-back with the clearly rising star Bob Hiller which was perfectly logical but had otherwise left well alone. Given there were only to be five Canadian matches in total they selected the incumbent front row comprising the captain Phil Judd, Steve Richards and Mike Coulman and merely added another Coventry prop in Jim Broderick plus John as the second hooker.

Perhaps he was not going as a back-up after all? A couple of warm-up games were arranged in the North and Midlands before the team set off and in one of them John had out-hooked Richards by a 7-0 margin. The tour was never going to be the most taxing as Canadian rugby was then very much a minority sport and indeed the tour ended without the England party conceding a single try.

Two easy wins were clocked up against regional teams in Calgary and over on Victoria Island before the single 'International' was staged in Vancouver at the large and rambling Empire Stadium which had hosted the 1954 Empire Games famous – or perhaps notorious – for where the British marathon runner Jim Peters had collapsed and nearly died within yards of the finishing line.

The match was not afforded full International status and as such never counted in a player's total of International caps although a unique special one was awarded for the tour. Having played at Victoria, John got the nod over Richards to play his full part in an easy 29-0 victory. Two further easy wins were then recorded in Toronto and Ottawa before the team returned to Britain to await the imminent arrival of the New Zealanders.

The Rugby Union in those days took the view that being selected for England was not only an honour but also something of a favour and that players could be treated by Committee men with the sort of high-handedness associated with 'officers and other ranks' in a Victorian army regiment.

On one occasion during the Canada tour several of the team had broken curfew the night before a match to go to a party and, returning to their twenty-storey hotel in the early hours of the morning, had elected to walk up all the fire escape rather than face getting caught by the management. A rather tired David Watt didn't fancy the climb and so pushed the lift button only to be met face-to-face by the team manager. The following morning it was deemed that the unfortunate Watty should be sent home although he was no more 'guilty' than a whole group of others. Captain Phil Judd had to make it abundantly clear that if one player was to be sent home for such a trifling event then they all would go with him and thus bring the tour to a highly embarrassing end. The matter was quietly dropped although Watt was not selected again for England for another five years. There were many examples of this prevailing attitude throughout the England career of John Pullin.

When they arrived a few weeks later, the All Blacks were led by Brian Lochore – a traditional Kiwi back-row man from Wairarapa – who had at his disposal virtually the entire squad which had demolished the Lions less than eighteen months earlier. This included a solid and aggressive hooker named Bruce McLeod who was backed up by another with a name probably more associated with the Houses of Parliament and perhaps cricket – John Major.

The All Blacks immediately slaughtered a scratch team from the north of England in Manchester at which point the selectors seemed to lose their nerve. A second scratch team rather clumsily entitled 'Midlands, London and Home Counties' was assembled to confront them at Leicester in a match that was to be soaked in tragedy. After just a few minutes the current England centre Danny Hearn hurled himself at his opposite number Ian MacRae and was left lying prone on the turf. Hearn had made quite a reputation for himself as a fearsome crash tackler and had done well in Canada but this time he got it slightly wrong with catastrophic results. He was carried off face down on a stretcher and very nearly died from his appalling spinal cord injury which has left him confined to a wheelchair for the past fifty years.

There were still no substitutes allowed and so the current England flanker Bob Taylor left the pack to replace Hearn in the backs and, as happens so often, the scratch pack of seven remaining forwards gelled together and gave their vaunted opponents a real battle. Although the match was lost the selectors, perhaps rashly, rushed out and announced that the entire pack – including the now veteran Godwin back at hooker – would face the All Blacks the following weekend before John, Rollitt or Watt could even make their case.

All three duly met the Tourists at Bristol the following Wednesday in another hastily assembled combination team called the 'South of England', which referred to just about anywhere south of The Wash and included John's pal Mike Collins on a wing. A familiar front row of Bev Dovey, John and Roger Grove (who had recently joined Leicester) out-hooked John Major 4-1 while Watt ensured a good share of the line-outs but elsewhere they were up against it and the visitors ran out the winners with three unanswered second-half tries.

Three days later England were comprehensively beaten by the wiles of the New Zealand half-back combination of Chris Laidlaw and Earle Kirton. The England pack struggled and no less than seven of them were dropped by the time of England's next match only ten weeks later and indeed five of them were never capped again. So much for consistent team building!

The All Blacks tore through Britain and France unbeaten although they were given a severe fright by the Barbarians at Twickenham. The hooking position for that titanic struggle was awarded to Scotland's Frank Laidlaw but John was destined to appear three more times for the famous club by the end of the season, taking in the traditional Boxing Day match at Leicester and a third consecutive Easter tour back in South Wales.

By early New Year two more wearisome Trials had been staged with the so-called 'second team' winning both times. Indeed, the final Trial held just two weeks before Wales were to return to Twickenham produced a complete selectors' nightmare when the England XV were yet again outplayed by 'The Rest' to the tune of 21-5, which at a time of a try being only worth three points would be considered to be comprehensive.

John was in that defeated England XV team alongside Judd and Horton and must have feared the worst as the selectors agonised over what sort of team to field. When it was finally announced they had come up with no less than eight new caps including two forwards who had very little senior experience to draw upon. Judd and Horton were both axed permanently but to his relief John had somehow retained the selectors' faith. One major comfort to him was that the new scrum- half was to be his club colleague Bill Redwood, the same man who had scored the winning try against Newport in John's first-team debut against Newport all that time ago.

Rather like that old saying about how a monkey with a typewriter would be able to produce the entire works of Shakespeare if given enough time, the selectors had somehow hit upon a pack which was to defy all the odds and perform extremely well throughout the succeeding four matches. It is perhaps worth recalling them as they played no small part in setting John up for all his many achievements over the following eight years.

In the front row with John were Mike Coulman – a powerful Staffordshire policeman who was considered particularly mobile for his era – and a virtually unknown student from Newcastle University called Brian Keen. As his name suggested, he proved to be willing and fit but at under 15 stone was never going to be a scrummaging sensation in the Horton mould. The locks were two very big men for the time in Peter Larter and Mike Parsons, both with Northampton, while the back row comprised Peter Bell who, though a new 'cap', had gained considerable experience with Blackheath, plus two relative babies in David Gay of Bath at Number 8 and a tall rangy teenager called Bryan West on the other flank. Both he and Coulman were later destined to sign to play Rugby League, which perhaps speaks for their running and passing skills if not for their set piece abilities.

So, on 20 January 1968, John embarked upon an unbroken run in the England team which was to last for seven years and glean him thirty-eight consecutive caps, a feat which at the time had never been achieved before. Wales also brought some new blood to Twickenham but were led by John's familiar adversary Norman Gale. John out-hooked Gale and England gained a draw at 11-11 in a match they might well have won. He did lose just one strike against the head (which his scrum-half Bill Redwood swears to this day was kicked out of his hands and never even reached the scrum) to allow the rising star that was Gareth Edwards to slide over for a snap try on the blind-side but, aside from that, Gale came off clearly second best and promptly lost his place to the aspiring Jeff Young for the coveted Welsh jersey.

Soon afterwards, Gloucestershire won the South West group of the County Championship rather belatedly by narrowly taking the final match against Cornwall at Redruth which had been postponed until the New Year due to an outbreak of foot-and-mouth disease. Having disposed of Oxfordshire, they then went down to Warwickshire (Herbie Godwin and all) at Coventry.

Away from rugby, 1968 will be remembered as a tempestuous year of political demonstrations, student riots, anti-Vietnam War protests and the birth of the hippy movement sandwiched as it was between the 'Summer of Love' in San Francisco the year before and Woodstock and all that went with it a year later. All that rock, acid and free love was a long way away from sheep farming and the England rugby team, although it is noticeable from the old photos at the time that John's neat parting had disappeared and that his hair was now becoming fashionably longer and shaggier.

It was also a year when there was to be a British Lions tour to South Africa and 1968 had also been a time when some uncomfortable truths about that country were beginning to draw headlines in the world press. On the positive side, Dr Christiaan Barnard had recently performed the first ever successful heart transplant, opening up a new avenue of hope for thousands worldwide, but on the other side the politics of apartheid were soon to force their way into the world of sport when Basil D'Oliveira was shamefully omitted from an England cricket team for a visit to South Africa. This was self-evidently on the grounds of his colour, sparking off a huge row which was to rock not only cricket but also rugby in particular for the next quarter of a century.

At that time the accepted practice was for a British Lions team (it was some years until the more politically correct 'British and Irish Lions' nomenclature was used) to travel with two teams making up thirty players and thus two hookers. Normally these would be two drawn from the current teams of the four competing nations although unavailability, injury and the occasional 'wild card' would sometimes affect this pattern. The leading hookers from each country were widely considered at the time to be Frank Laidlaw of Scotland, Ken Kennedy of Ireland (both of whom had been to New Zealand with the Lions two years before), Norman Gale or Jeff Young from Wales and now John himself.

It was at this point that John began to thank his stars for the loyal and unflinching support of his father and in particular his two brothers. It was never easy for amateur players to absent themselves for almost four months at a time with careers, professional examinations and family commitments looming large and for farmers this posed huge potential problems. However, time and again the family rallied around and John was able to tour the world confident that all was well back at the farm. In John's case there was an added pressure as he and Brenda were by then due to become parents for the first time and their first daughter Mandy was to be born later that year. Again, Brenda selflessly supported him in his being able to make himself available as she was to do so many times in the future. Not all players were quite so lucky.

Having gained both of his caps against the Welsh, his next England match was against Ireland and for once the England team was announced as unchanged. This time England were definitely unlucky not to have won as, early on, Bill Redwood was badly concussed and finally taken off before half-time. As in the All Blacks match at Leicester there were still no replacements allowed and Peter Bell – a bulky back-row man – was pressed into service as a makeshift scrum-half and was understandably way out of his comfort zone. John also picked up a nagging back injury which was to trouble him for quite a while, although it did not actually prevent him from playing. For all that a second draw was claimed in a rather dour match in which Tom Kiernan kicked three penalty goals for Ireland with Bob Hiller replying with two for England coupled with a drop goal from Moseley's John Finlan.

A key point in John's favour was that Kennedy was sidelined throughout the Championship after a recent knee operation and thus would not be available for the Lions and his replacement Aidan Brady, although clearly very competent, was unlikely to be in serious contention. The prospect of a Lion's place was beginning to look rosier.

The next game followed only a fortnight later at the old Stade at Colombes in the communist-minded township of that name on the outskirts of Paris. It had a long and proud history including hosting the 1924 Olympic Games of *Chariots of Fire* fame and had even hosted an Olympic Rugby Final implausibly won by the United States. This was following a huge brawl with the French after which the sport was kicked out of the Games for virtually a century on the basis that Baron de Coubertin felt that it engendered hooliganism. Since then it had hosted the 1938 Football World Cup and every rugby and football international France had played for decades.

By 1968 it was way past its prime, away from the more prestigious parts of Paris and incapable of taking more than around 40,000 in any degree of comfort. France had fought a bitter war of a match against the All Blacks and had run them very close but the sport was reeling from the recent deaths of two of their star backs, Guy Boniface and Jean Capendeguy, in separate road accidents. For all of that they had an extremely powerful team featuring the Camberabero brothers at half-back who had an almost psychic understanding of one another's moves, the exciting Jean Gachassin as an experienced centre and the great Walter Spanghero in the pack. They were to win all four matches to obtain the elusive 'Grand Slam' for the first time but England gave them a good run for their money.

With an unchanged pack and a couple of tweaks in the backs including replacing the luckless Redwood with the previous year's scrum-half Roger Pickering, England went into an early lead and had a try by winger Keith Savage mysteriously disallowed but were finally overtaken in the second half. Again, John was fortunate with his opposing hookers as the highly experienced Jean-Michel Cabanier had been jettisoned by the French selectors for a virtually unknown new cap called Michel Yachvili, a name to reappear a generation later.

England's final match was to be fought out at Murrayfield after which the Lions' selectors would have to come up with their final choices. Once again John had a little stroke of good fortune in that Frank Laidlaw had to withdraw due to injury and yet another new cap named Derek Deans – a famous surname for hookers from Hawick – was drafted into the side. It was another close affair with fly-half Mike Weston seemingly kicking the leather off the ball in his final International but England finally prevailed thanks to a rampaging try from Mike Coulman coming around the back of a line-out to smash his way over.

Given the unpromising start with the All Black defeat and the shambolic Trials process, the England forwards had proved both mobile and durable and had remained unchanged for the first time in eight years and ended the season in mid-table, which might not impress modern rugby followers but at the time was a considerable improvement. Several England players might be justified in putting their hands up for selection for the Lions. John just had to hope he would turn out to be one of the fortunate ones.

11

On Trek with the Lions

When the British Lions team to tour South Africa was finally announced John was delighted to see his name among the party of thirty players and two officials to make the trip. He cannot have been particularly surprised as he had performed consistently well in an England team which had probably done rather better than might have been expected over the four Internationals that winter.

The two officials were the manager, David Brooks, a man who, although never having played at the very top level himself, had been a prominent member of the Harlequins and probably more relevantly had recently managed a tour by the club to South Africa and hence had a fair idea of what to expect, and the Irish ex-Lions skipper Ronnie Dawson, who was given the title of 'assistant manager' but was effectively the coach. Furthermore, Dawson had himself been a world-class hooker and had captained Ireland against South Africa both in Dublin and out in Cape Town, which would hopefully ensure a thorough understanding of just what might occur with a Springbok front row.

The selected party was to be led by the highly experienced Tom Kiernan who had already toured South Africa twice before and included some exciting young Welsh backs including Gareth Edwards, Gerald Davies, Barry John, Maurice Richards and the somewhat mercurial Keith Jarrett. These were to be joined by Ireland's often brilliant Mike Gibson plus Scots Jock Turner and Sandy Hinshelwood who had been one of the Lions' precious few successes two years before in New Zealand.

As for the pack, the selectors were acutely conscious that they would need to meet the Springboks toe-to-toe up front and had put an emphasis on physical size and power – perhaps to the detriment of pace. Indeed, the back row was to become something of an Achilles heel as the tour wore on, not least because the selectors, in their wisdom, had opted to take one extra three-quarter and only pick five back-row men.

John was delighted to see that the selectors had ignored their English counterparts and were taking his favourite tight-head Tony Horton as well as the vastly experienced Irishman Syd Millar, the powerful Cardiff man John O'Shea and his English loose-head prop Mike Coulman. The locks comprised the indestructible Willie John McBride who was also returning to South Africa, England's Peter Larter, Llanelli's Delme Thomas and the enormous Peter Stagg who, at around 6 feet 10 inches, was at that time the tallest man to have ever stepped onto a top-level rugby field. The back row by contrast was on the small side, comprising the aggressive Scot Jim Telfer, Northampton's Bob Taylor (another man mysteriously ignored by England selectors), his namesake the Watford Welshman John Taylor, Irishman Mick Doyle and a surprising selection in the relatively inexperienced Roger Arneil. As often happens Arneil blossomed and became one of the outstanding forwards on the tour. The most surprising omission appeared to be the big and mobile Irish Number 8 Ken Goodall.

In those days the Lions met for pre-tour training at Eastbourne College, thus giving the party the chance to get to know each other and for the press to get in as many interviews and photographs as they could. Prop John O'Shea recalled,

> We were all weighed and measured and a couple of days later, our outfits of two blazers, shirts, trousers and ties arrived. We could also buy track-suits if we wished but there were then no official Lions tracksuits on offer. The Scottish knitwear firm Pringle also supplied us all with smart blue sweaters with the Lions logo. Our daily allowance was only ten bob each although we rarely had to put our hands in our pockets for a drink.

The tour was already going to be politically controversial not only because of the growing awareness of the apartheid policy being rigidly enforced in South Africa but also because it was going to include what was then still known as Rhodesia. Three years earlier talks between their elected leader Ian Smith and Prime Minister Harold Wilson had collapsed acrimoniously and Rhodesia had issued a Unilateral Declaration of Independence. Since then they had been summarily kicked out of the Commonwealth and had been subject to various economic sanctions. This was surely going test David Brooks's diplomatic skills to the limit. He soon found his own unique way of dealing with it.

The other hooker was to be Jeff Young who had only recently taken over from Norman Gale and was serving in the RAF and, while stationed in Yorkshire, was currently playing his club rugby for Harrogate. Young was a fraction smaller than John and a couple of years younger but was a tough nugget of a man who often chose to hook with his nearer (left) foot on his own team's put-in and in John's words 'had the reputation among referees as being a bit of a cheat in the scrums and used to get penalised rather a lot'.

Before leaving, the party were to be addressed by an official from the South African embassy who were becoming acutely conscious of the prevailing attitude in the UK with regard to their apartheid regime. His approach was dismissive to say the least as his short address on the subject ran along the lines of, 'The rugby is great, the women are great but the politics you just won't understand.' Not particularly helpful.

The party flew out and pitched into a week of training at a place called Stilfontein, which is a small mining town on the Transvaal close to Potchefstroom where the first match against Western Transvaal was due to be played. It was here that the first indication of the prevailing attitude was brought home forcibly to flanker John Taylor who recalled,

> Some white farmers came in and began sounding off loudly in the most violent terms about the non-whites and treated the people working in the hotel abominably and it just carried on from there. At the time I was teaching in Putney at what was even back then a happy multi-racial school and I could hardly believe my ears.

Taylor was so affected by the whole environment that two years later he refused to play against the Springboks and in doing so temporarily lost his place in the Wales team.

John sat that first match out but then made his Lions debut four days later at the historic Newlands ground in Cape Town against Western Province. He was fortunate to have Millar and Horton beside him as the pack was going to be sorely tested before finally running out 10-6 winners.

As the players got to know one another a little better, Tony Horton mentioned to John that he and his wife had recently bought a house in a pretty country village with a field attached and that he had purchased a few sheep to 'keep the grass down'. His wife Angela was a glamorous model for Norman Hartnell and thus a little bit of a 'townie' and they both thought you could just leave the sheep to their own devices as though they were still in the wild. 'When you get back they will all be dead' was John's deadpan reply. Cue some frantic phone calls back from South Africa as to watering, injections and all the other things the poor girl now had to contend with.

One of the perennial bugbears of overseas tours was the fact that the home countries and indeed home regions invariably supplied the referee who, without any supporting technology, was the sole man in charge. Furthermore, there were several small but important differences in how the laws of the game were interpreted in different parts of the world. This certainly included the grey areas of hooking and both John and Jeff Young suffered badly in this respect, which in turn inevitably led to serious difficulties and accusations from touring teams of 'home town bias'. Even if the man in the middle had the most honourable intentions – and the majority almost certainly did – this could rapidly cause all sorts of problems.

That tour was also the first occasion when it had been permissible to replace an injured player in an International or tour match but, even then, only on the say-so of a doctor on the touchline who again was appointed by the home team. Furthermore, a reserve was expected to sit in the stand in his normal clothing and only go and change for the match once the touchline 'quack' had given his diagnosis. This nearly cost the Lions the match in Cape Town when both Taylors – Bob and John – sustained ligament injuries but were informed that they were fit to return to the field only to hobble around painfully doing themselves further damage in the process.

John's next game was a week later against Eastern Province in Port Elizabeth where he had a hand in a try by Bob Hiller in a match which the Lions were fortunate to win. The next stop was by the seaside in Durban for a more convincing win over Natal. It had begun well for John and he was 6-1 up in the scrum count until his trick of slipping his bind on his loose-head prop for once failed him and he strained his left shoulder painfully. He then lost the next three scrums until the final whistle signalled a 17-5 victory.

This annoying injury was not a serious one but effectively ruled him out of the First Test which was due to take place in Pretoria the following Saturday. Injuries are an inevitable problem in rugby and never more so than on a long tour on hard-baked grounds against massively motivated opponents. With hindsight it seems incredible that the Lions travelled with no medical or physiotherapy support whatsoever and had to rely often upon cack-handed treatment from local hospitals.

In John Reason's book of the tour he illustrated the point vividly:

> The casual treatment the Lions received was erratic to say the least. John Pullin once limped into a surgery for treatment for a blackened toe, and after a red-hot rod had been thrust to the bone, found he could not walk at all!

Just before the First Test the team made that detour up to Rhodesia. It is now known that manager David Brooks had been sent a letter by Diplomatic Bag from the Foreign Office in London requesting that the Lions should refuse to go there. Rather like Nelson putting his telescope to his blind eye, Brooks (who had a shrewd idea what it might contain) declined to open it until they actually arrived in Harare – then still known as Salisbury. Unsurprisingly they were warmly welcomed by the recalcitrant prime minister, Ian Smith, and the brief visit and comfortable victory turned out to be one big party and one of the highlights of the tour.

That First Test in Pretoria was lost only narrowly by 20-25 although the Springboks scored three tries to the Lions' single one from McBride. Tom Kiernan kept the Lions in the hunt by landing five penalty goals but the injury list continued to grow. Barry John's collar bone was cracked so badly as to rule him out of the rest of the tour. His replacement, Mike Gibson, was then forced to run down to the dressing room below the stand tearing off his clothes as he went to change frantically into his kit before finally arriving onto the pitch with no warm up a whole fifteen minutes later. In doing so he thus became the first replacement in international history.

Just before the end Jeff Young was carried off on a stretcher having been run over not once but twice by an entire rampant Springbok pack after a scrum had collapsed. Tony Horton recalled, 'It was brutal, the Springboks not only heeled the ball out of the back of the scrum but our hooker as well!' John probably felt somewhat relieved to have missed out on all that.

As one might expect John was his usual quiet and unassuming self but as the tour progressed the team forged itself into a close band of brothers and they remain so until this day. O'Shea, who was among the more extrovert members of the team, recalled,

He was never on the sidelines on his own and joined in with the singing and the 'Players Court' which was held every weekend at which I, as presiding judge, would have miscreants brought trembling before me. The prosecuting counsels were usually Gerald Davies and Syd Millar. At one of these John was found guilty of the heinous crime of being 'too well behaved' so I made him stand in the corner.

All rugby men on a long tour need to let off a bit of steam and there were any number of pranks dreamed up to relieve the boredom of the continual treadmill of playing, travelling and recovering from various injuries and ailments.

Whilst the rugby was invariably hard and sometimes brutal the South African public were hospitable to a fault. One particularly generous host was an ex-England fly-half and British Lion named Jeff Reynolds who had met a local girl on the 1938 tour and had returned to South Africa after the war to marry her and run a hotel near Cape Town. Nothing was too much trouble to the extent of him supplying an oversized bed for the nearly 7-foot-tall Peter Stagg.

One day the Lions returned to find Jeff was away and the bar was shut – hence no beer. One intrepid soul traced the connecting pipe to the cellars and managed to cut it so that they now had all the beer they could possibly get down their throats and also for free. When Reynolds returned he took it all without batting an eyelid and manager Brooks later paid up cheerfully for both the beer and any damage to the pipe.

In fact, if there was going to be any high jinks it was highly likely that the tour manager was going to be one of the instigators rather than the dour disciplinarian which had been the case on previous occasions and indeed on a few since. Fifty years later many of those players still recall that tour as probably the best they had ever been on from the point of view of fun.

Bob Hiller who, apart from being a superb full-back and goal-kicker, was known for his quick-witted repartee, divided the tourists into the 'Kippers' (those such as Jim Telfer and John who always liked to get a good night's sleep) and the 'Wreckers' who enjoyed nothing more than going around tipping the Kippers out of bed in the middle of the night.

One of the Wreckers was Willie John McBride who had a few whimsical ideas of his own. Outside the front door of one hotel he started a 'magic bonfire' and everybody who had to pass was 'encouraged' by the giant Irishman to donate a piece of their clothing into the flames to 'sustain the magic'. Various ties and socks kept it going until a very smartly dressed young couple who were nothing to do with the Lions emerged probably on their way to a dinner dance. Fair play to them the only things they could donate without it being immediately noticeable were a couple of items of their underwear and duly complied to Willie John's evident approval. Clearly the magic worked for the Lions went on an unbeaten run right up to the First Test.

John was fit to return in Windhoek against what is now known as Namibia but then merely as South West Africa and then for an eagerly anticipated match at Ellis Park in Johannesburg against Transvaal. It was here that John and his scrum-half Roger Young ran into their first major problems with a home town referee. Mr Koos Stander seemed to wage his own private war on the Lions' scrum and John was hauled up for foot up, swinging, striking outside the scrum and just about anything else the wretched man could dream up whilst his scrum-half suffered more or less the same fate. As a result, Transvaal had ten shots at goal and the result finished as British Lions 6 Transvaal 14. It was an acutely frustrating experience for all concerned and was the only Provincial match to be lost throughout the entire tour.

On a happier note John was able to claim his place in the team for the Second Test back in Port Elizabeth. He recalled the match easily: 'In my whole career I have never experienced physical pressure like it before or since. Their two props Myburgh and Marais scrummaged so low and with such force that it was hard to breathe let alone move.'

Once again John and his scrum-half Gareth Edwards ran into a series of extraordinarily one-sided refereeing decisions, this time by a man named Dr Strasheim. He had taken no action when fly-half Mike Gibson had been flattened by Frik du Preez whilst miles away from the ball but had then persecuted the Lions front row to the extent that at one point John decided not to hook at all rather than incur yet another penalty kick. It was a great pity as the Lions did well and the match finished as a draw.

All this triggered off a bit of a crisis as Strasheim had been appointed by the all-powerful Dr Craven despite the fact that he was not even on the International Panel and had now been widely condemned as being appalling. One newspaper even reported that David Brooks was so incensed that he had threatened to take the team home. This was perhaps a bit exaggerated but the fact remains that the Lions only rated two of the referees they encountered on the entire tour. Max Baise and Walter Lane were the two honourable exceptions to a thoroughly disreputable general rule.

John was probably glad to have missed the next match at the small town of Springs in which Jeff Young got into a running battle with the local Eastern Transvaal hooker – yet again sparked off by wildly different refereeing interpretations of the hooking rules. At one point all hell was let loose as John O'Shea waded into the opposing pack throwing punches like a whirling dervish and was promptly sent off. As he left the field to a shower of missiles a bespectacled spectator unwisely tried to attack him only to be soundly belted in the face by Willie John McBride who had joined Tony Horton from the sidelines in coming to rescue O'Shea. One way or another it was not an edifying business.

It would be wrong to portray the whole tour as a litany of violence as the South Africans were invariably hospitable although there was often something of a language barrier with the Afrikaans-speaking communities. However, just as Mike Gibson had been punched senseless in the Second Test, the next one at Cape Town saw John as the victim.

Ten days earlier the Lions had run out narrow winners in what was often referred to as the 'Fifth Test' against the famed Blue Bulls of Northern Transvaal in Pretoria who had always prided themselves upon having some of the most powerful scrummagers anywhere in the world. Along with Coulman and the immediately reinstated O'Shea, John had found it predictably 'highly competitive' against the current Springbok hooker Gys Pitzer.

The Third Test in Cape Town ultimately decided the series in favour of South Africa as they won 11-6 with a try from flanker Thys Lourens separating the sides. In the first few minutes the Lions scrum was severely disrupted when Mike Coulman damaged ankle ligaments when fielding a Springbok drop-out. Horton had to move across to loose-head with McBride moving up to prop until another lock, Delme Thomas, came on as a replacement to act as a makeshift prop. Horton confessed that he had never played at loose-head before in his life having arrived as a specialist tight-head prop via the unlikely route of full-back, centre and flanker. John just had to accept all the slings and arrows of misfortune in his usual stoical manner and the cobbled-together front row performed remarkably well and never lost a single scrum on their own ball.

At one point, and at a short line-out, John pinned his opposite number, Pitzer, into the front of it in the approved method of the time but, as the ball moved away, was smashed from behind by a cheap shot haymaker from Pitzer which temporarily laid him out cold. It was all caught on a BBC film and later played back in slow motion but the officials, local press and indeed the Springbok selectors all chose to turn a blind eye to the incident. What John O'Shea must have thought of all this can only be imagined!

John played his full part in a win over the Orange Free State in Bloemfontein but, as the Final Test approached, was struck down with flu and was sent to bed with a high temperature. Perhaps unwisely, he declared himself fit to play on the morning of the match and for once gave an under-par performance in a game that was won decisively by South Africa 19-6 scoring four tries to none in the process.

Notwithstanding the occasional outbreaks of foul play and several cases of abysmal refereeing the tour was generally reckoned to have been moderately successful. Apart from the farce against Transvaal all the provincial matches were won and although the Test rubber was lost 0-1-3 it was only in the very last match that they were beaten decisively. Happily, there had been no diplomatic incidents despite all the colour bar problems and the delicate visit to Ian Smith's Rhodesia.

Off the pitch they had indulged in plenty of fun as the tales of the Kippers and the Wreckers would testify. These of course were mainly just harmless high jinks but if and when matters were ever to go any further than that, we go back again to that old maxim in rugby of 'what goes on tour stays on tour' and even after half a century this should be respected.

Unlike the sensation-seeking hacks of today who are desperate for any dirt that can be dug up, the British press of that time were all true rugby men who travelled and mixed freely with the players and were perfectly happy to draw a veil over anything which might cause embarrassment back home. Some snippets nevertheless reached the South African press (who loved any opportunity to have a 'pop' at the opposition) about wrecked hotel rooms, drunken binges, people being tipped out of their bunks on overnight trains and various other real, exaggerated or just imaginary bacchanalian escapades.

None of this ever seemed to involve John. One imagines that he merely shrugged his broad shoulders, sipped his beer and just left them to get on with it.

12

A Candle in the Wind

Back in February 1960 our then prime minister, Harold MacMillan, on a widely reported Commonwealth tour, had addressed a somewhat uncomfortable South African parliament about what he had just seen in West Africa and alluded to the impending rush towards independence of many erstwhile colonial states. His memorable phrase was that a 'wind of change' was sweeping across Africa and that there was very little that could or indeed should be done to prevent it.

A decade later much of this had come to pass, although the two main rugby-playing nations in Africa – Rhodesia and South Africa – had still clung onto white-minority rule and had, if anything, tightened their grip to try to hold on against that prevailing racial wind which was by then keeping them awake at night.

Coincidentally the sport of Rugby Union was also beginning to get caught up in the same crosswinds. A new generation of players, born during or just after the war, never having had to undertake National Service and having spent their teenage years in the increasingly libertarian 'swinging sixties,' were becoming less and less inclined to touch their forelocks to the old guard of rugby administrators. These ultra-conservative men (and they were exclusively male) sought to somehow keep things just as they had always been: traditional, unstructured and, above all, fanatically amateur.

But the world around them was slowly but inexorably changing. John's generation had grown up at a time when coaching was unknown and frankly frowned upon but, by the late 1960s, Peter Colston had assumed just that role at Bristol and clubs all over the country were rapidly following suit. National and county-based cup competitions had begun to spring up and the rapid growth of new universities ensured that Oxford and Cambridge would no longer be the only source of graduate players into International rugby. On top of this the arrival of affordable air fares allowed even modest club teams to tour as far afield as Kenya and Bermuda rather than just Cornwall and Devon.

Over the next few seasons the use of replacements was beginning to filter down from the International matches (such as the farce of Gibson's mad dash to change in Pretoria) into club rugby when John's own experience in the first minute of a televised Cup Final was soon to hasten the process. The laws of the game now restricted direct kicking into touch outside of a kicker's 22-metre line, and this had been as much to do with making the game more attractive to spectators as anything else.

With an eye to players' daytime jobs and the constant paranoia about covert 'professionalism', International teams were still forbidden from meeting before the Thursday immediately prior to the match itself and any other training sessions were banned. This may help to explain why touring teams to the United Kingdom won so many matches: they were just less disorganised.

At one point it was discovered that Wales were quietly having get-togethers at the Afan Lido just outside Port Talbot and the England players began to do the same on certain Sundays with the forwards somehow miraculously bumping into one another in Coventry with the backs doing likewise at the same time in Northampton. The RFU must have been aware of all this and looked the other way but, in time-honoured fashion, refused to reimburse the players for any travelling expenses. John's deadpan comment was, 'I wondered why they picked Starmer-Smith at scrum-half. Starmer can be running around with the backs at Northampton while Smith works with us on our set-pieces in Coventry.'

One other change spread rapidly through the sport and that was the practice of the hooker being designated to throw the ball into the line-out. Today this is virtually universal and an otherwise good hooker and general forward can easily find himself dropped if his throwing-in fails to pass muster. This was not always the case and John readily admits it was never his strongest point and that he never really liked having to do it.

The Bristol club could lay claim to being the pioneers of this. When Peter Colston had captained the club, he had inherited an experienced core of players and wisely chose to follow a fairly democratic approach which allowed his men to contribute fully and try out all sorts of ideas on the field. In the same way that

John could generally guarantee a major share of the ball from the set scrums the 6 feet and 6 inches of David Watt could be relied upon to provide a steady stream of line-out progression – provided he received an accurate throw and Watty was not averse to having a good old moan if he didn't receive it.

In the mid-1960s Bristol's wingers were the very quick Mike Ellery and Mike Collins but, try as they might, throwing-in was not their strong point. One evening at training prop Roger Grove volunteered that he was quite good at darts and proceeded to throw a number of perfect deliveries to the grateful Watty. The captain immediately twigged that this would release one of his speedy wingers to produce either an overlap or a decoy run outside his fly-half and the practice was adopted. Better still the jumpers would enjoy the consistency of working with only one thrower and the released winger could also act as a second full-back if required. Some special short line-out moves were soon developed which involved Grove following in and then peeling around the front and in doing so he claimed several tries in the process.

Grove subsequently moved to Leicester and in due course Colston became Bristol's first official coach but by then the job devolved permanently onto the hookers, which of course included John. By the beginning of the 1970s the practice had become almost universal. Because John never enjoyed this new aspect of a hooker's duties, prop Mike Fry often took over the responsibility for this whenever John was back turning out for Bristol.

On the International field an outstanding generation of Welsh players were to dominate the then Five Nations for several years with France generally not too far behind. Wales had the distinct advantage of pioneering properly organised coaching through deep-thinking rugby men such as Ray Williams, Roy Bish, John Robins and the brilliant Carwyn James. Furthermore, was it just a coincidence that their clubs had a more liberal attitude to paying generous expenses to their best players? Perhaps not. But there was no question that the more conservative nations of Scotland, Ireland and England seemed to struggle by comparison.

John's rugby career had ended by the time that League structures, World Cups and finally the advent of professionalism came to pass but during the second half of his career, from around 1968 until the mid-1970s, all those winds of change had certainly begun to blow.

Between John returning from visiting South Africa with the Lions in 1968 and returning there as a triumphant captain four years later England's dismal record read as having played nineteen of which a mere five had been won with one draw and thirteen lost – in several cases by twenty-point margins. This was indeed a dark period, yet through all this litany of combined failure he had become widely recognised as the best hooker in the sport – a brightly flickering candle of light in an otherwise dark and windy world.

Of course, he was not alone and, despite their setbacks, the England selectors were able to bring in some notable new faces, especially in the forwards with talented young men such as Tony Neary, Andy Ripley, Chris Ralston, Fran Cotton, Stack Stevens and Peter Dixon moulding into a formidable unit. Conversely, they never seemed to be able to settle upon a consistent half-back combination nor a centre partnership for more than a tiny handful of games before they wielded the axe once again following yet another humiliating defeat.

This was equally true of the captaincy as it was to be passed around like a ticking time bomb between Dick Greenwood, Budge Rogers, Bob Hiller, Bob Taylor, John Spencer, Bob Hiller (again) and finally Peter Dixon before the selectors finally turned to their quiet and undemonstrative hooker almost as a desperate last throw of the dice.

John had returned from the tour of South Africa with a sky-high reputation but physically and emotionally fairly drained. He had also endured a shoulder injury, a bad bout of flu and being knocked cold by the irascible Mr Pitzer. In those amateur days it was generally accepted that a player returning from a long tour overseas would take two or three months off from rugby to catch up on work and family matters (John was soon to become a father for the first time), recover from the physical and mental battering from all the often brutally hard matches, the endless and wearisome travel and generally living in an artificial 'goldfish bowl' for weeks on end.

John's family had lovingly covered his absence from the farm but there was inevitably much to be attended to. Furthermore, he and Brenda had never before been apart for such a long time and now there was a baby daughter to consider as well. It was a time to recharge his batteries and get rid of all the accumulated aches and pains before taking the field again.

He returned to training in early November and then eased himself back into action via a couple of games with the United team. Gloucestershire had dipped out to Cornwall in the South West group in his absence and when the first England Trial took place just before Christmas he was still not fully ready. While he stood back from the game down in Falmouth the local hooker Roger Harris stepped into his place.

The annual Barbarians match at Leicester was postponed due to the weather but John did make it to the next Trial up at West Hartlepool where he appeared in a 'Probables' win over a 'Possibles' team which included, for the first time, a fellow farmer from Cornwall who was in due course to become his favourite loose-head prop and lifelong friend – Stack Stevens. He missed the final Trial where yet again the England XV lost decisively to The Rest to once more throw selection into the melting pot. While you could never be quite sure (given the caprice of selection committees), John was probably more or less guaranteed his place.

The opening fixture was against Ireland and the team which travelled to Dublin contained three exciting new three-quarters in the persons of the lightning-quick Keith Fielding and the much-admired centre pairing of John Spencer and David Duckham whilst the pack now featured the tall and feisty policeman Nigel Horton and an ebullient fruit and vegetable merchant named Keith Fairbrother. The story goes that when Dicky Jeeps, a selector, fruit farmer and thus one of Fairbrother's many suppliers, saw the new prop roar into the car park in his shiny new E-type Jaguar he remarked, 'Obviously you're not paying me enough for my bloody apples.'

It turned out to be an exciting match with John packing down against a fit-again Ken Kennedy. The Irish scraped home by a mere two points and England might just have snatched a win at the death had Hiller not just failed with a penalty shot from halfway into a biting wind. For the first time John was to have a Bristol colleague alongside with Dave Rollitt recalled at Number 8.

An unchanged team was announced for the next match at Twickenham although Will Greenwood's father Dick – who had led the team in Dublin – was forced to withdraw the night before having injured an eye playing squash. It was not a serious injury and only a fortnight later he was leading Lancashire to win the County Championship down at Redruth, but he was never to be selected for England again. It was indeed a bizarre way to finish an International career. The captaincy thus passed to Budge Rogers, who was to break the England record for total caps and hold it until it was broken by John himself some five years later.

The French fielded a much-changed team and included another virtually unknown debutant hooker of Polish descent named Christian Swierczinski. As all rugby followers well know the French can be maddeningly unpredictable and now flopped from being Grand Slam winners the previous year to propping up the table. England, for whom Rollitt scored a fine try near a corner flag, won the match at something of a canter with John out-hooking his new rival to such an extent that the unfortunate newcomer never again appeared in a Five Nations match.

An unchanged team then narrowly defeated the Scots at Twickenham. The Scots' front row was comprised of debutant Ian McLauchlan, Frank Laidlaw and Sandy Carmichael, all of whom were to join John on his second Lions tour two years later. Laidlaw had built up quite a reputation over the past five years as a small but resourceful hooker and although John came out marginally ahead in the set scrums, it was a much tougher contest than had been the case with the French. One notable occurrence was that England used a replacement for the first time when winger Fielding picked up an ankle injury to be replaced by Tim Dalton of Coventry who was a fly-half but was thus destined to spend his entire England career lasting only fifty minutes playing way out of position. To his credit he managed to produce a slick wrap-around pass to his club colleague David Duckham to claim the try which won the match.

Meanwhile John had resumed his love affair with the Barbarians when the postponed match at Leicester was finally played. The Baa-Baas had a surprisingly easy time of it, winning the match by 35-0 with the voracious Duckham claiming no less than five tries. A month later John was pulling on the famous black and white shirt yet again for the annual Edgar Mobbs memorial match at Northampton but this time the boot was very much on the other foot as they were thrashed 3-23 by the East Midlands.

By this time John was becoming something of a West Country celebrity and it had its benefits. One of the other Bristol men selected for that match was the young Cornish winger Ken Plummer who recalled,

> We came back from Northampton in my car and I was doing the driving. I got pulled over by a police car in the middle of Cirencester and thought I was about to get a speeding ticket when one of the cops recognised John, tore up the ticket and sent us merrily on our way.

He now received an invitation from the Barbarians to make a second successive trip to South Africa immediately after the end of the season. Unlike the Lions tour the previous summer it would only last around three weeks but would again include a match in Harare (still called Salisbury) at the end of the tour. Again, thanks to the support he was enjoying from his brothers and Brenda he was able to accept.

Because of building work on the stadium, the match with Wales at Cardiff had been switched from its traditional date in January to the middle of April, no doubt with the added hope of avoiding the mudbaths which had so often reduced these eagerly awaited clashes to something of a farce. Wales had just come off the back of a draw in Paris and in the light of England's two recent victories the team travelled down to Cardiff with a fair degree of optimism. This turned out to be sorely misplaced.

Since John's debut against the Welsh three years before preparation for matches was as haphazard as ever and the powers that be persisted in seemingly frowning upon any practice sessions beyond a gentle run-out, practising a few line-out calls, a couple of set moves in the backs, etc.

David Powell recalled wistfully, 'The RFU actually used to put guards on the gates of the Lensbury Club to somehow ensure that we didn't turn up early for training and so risk being declared professional.' You couldn't make stuff like that up!

Rogers was thus condemned to carry out a secretive extra evening session on a remote pitch with the only light coming from car headlights. The intense scientific preparation of modern teams seems like coming from another world.

John would have been pleased to have been joined by a third Bristol teammate when Ken Plummer was drafted in to replace the injured Fielding, but it turned out to be a very chastening experience not only for Plummer but the entire England team. The old Arms Park still had the builders in and only three sides of the stadium were in use with the crowd thus limited to around 30,000, but the confident Welsh gave them a real treat.

Wales were on the cusp of a sustained period of domination with a fine and generally settled team which now featured the lanky Mervyn Davies in the back row and the rock-like J. P. R. Williams coming in at full-back. The England pack struggled to compete until half-time, after which the dam burst as the rampant Welshmen ran in five tries of which no less than four came from left wing Maurice Richards. The England pack were by then completely subjugated and with Barry John gorging himself on a metronomic service from his Cardiff partner Gareth Edwards, John Dawes repeatedly manufactured gaping overlaps to leave the luckless Ken Plummer clutching at thin air.

John and his props Powell and Fairbrother had done well for the first three matches but this time they had no real answers either. All in all, it was a thoroughly depressing afternoon from an English perspective. However, it was now time to put all that behind and meet up with the Barbarians and get back on the plane for the long flight to Johannesburg.

The Barbarians took only twenty-three players on the trip including Frank Laidlaw and John as the two hookers with John O'Shea, Keith Fairbrother and Norman Suddon of Hawick as the only three props. Frank and John shared the hooking duties, each appearing in three of the six games. Laidlaw appeared in an opening convincing victory over an invitation team called The Quaggas with John coming in for a narrow defeat in Durban against a strong Natal team followed by another against South Africa's own version of the Barbarians in Port Elizabeth.

The previous year he had been carrying an injury when the Lions had visited Rhodesia but this time, under the captaincy of 'Tess' O'Shea, he played his part in an exciting 24-21 victory. As a private club the Barbarians could cheerfully ignore any Foreign Office interference and John particularly enjoyed his time there where they were housed and entertained in relatively sumptuous style.

By that time, he was getting to know the South Africans pretty well and the relationship was due to continue.

Right: Eileen Pullin with her three young sons, 1949. John is on the left.

Below: Bill and Eileen Pullin with sons John (left), Phillip (centre) and Jeffrey (right), 1958.

Above: Early days at Bristol. Derek Neate captains the team with John standing back left.

Below left: John, by now a Bristol 1st XV regular.

Below right: Making friends with a young lamb.

Above left: After ten to twelve hours of heavy farm work training seemed like a rest.

Above right: With the letter 'I' on his back, John practises line-out throwing at Bristol.

Below: Training with the 1968 British Lions.

A hunting party in South Africa with fellow Lions Roger Young, Bob Hiller, Keith Jarrett and (kneeling) Tony Horton.

Returning to South Africa with the Barbarians. John is second left on the back row.

Offloading the ball against the South African Barbarians at Port Elizabeth.

A December 1969 England front row with Fairbrother and Stevens.

Above: The day John scored the winning try for England v South Africa. *Back Row*: David Duckham, Martin Hale, Bryan West, Peter Larter, Keith Fairbrother, Tony Bucknall, Stack Stevens, Roger Shackleton, Nigel Starmer-Smith. *Front Row*: John Spencer, John Pullin, Bob Hiller (capt.), Mike Davis, Keith Fielding, Bob Taylor.

Left: Haphazard practice session before an England game in 1972. John inexplicably jumps for a ball amongst a jumble of ill-matched training kits.

Above: Barbarians in 1970 on another enjoyable Easter weekend in Wales.

Right: On the run against Wales in Cardiff. Fran Cotton tries to catch up.

Above left: Daughter Mandy in a Lions shirt.

Above right: Painful aftermath of the Cup Final against Coventry in 1973.

Bristol v London Welsh at the Memorial Ground.

1972 and the team which shook the Springboks when John led England for the first time.

John Watkins wields a native weapon in South Africa. Knight, Palmer, John and Stevens look suitably unimpressed.

Above left: Fishing trip in New Zealand with Mike Roberts and Frank Laidlaw.

Above right: A first pony for Mandy and Jonathan.

Below: Gloucestershire play Middlesex at Richmond.

Above: A favourite West Country front row of Burton, Pullin and Stevens.

Right: The conquering hero returns from South Africa.

The two mates Pullin and Stevens on a quiet moment in New Zealand.

Calm before the storm. Lining up to meet Fiji at Gloucester in the 'dirtiest match I ever played in'.

Three Pullin brothers at a wedding.

Leading England against Australia at Twickenham.

A farmer has the chance to see more of his children than most city workers.

Lost in a crowd after beating the All Blacks in Auckland.

The last International when recalled against France in Paris 1976.

A West Country sportsman's award ceremony.

Life after rugby. John and Brenda could spend more time together.

Headshot.

13

Springbok Revenge

Following on from the Lions and Barbarians tours of South Africa, the Springboks fulfilled a long-standing visit to the UK and Ireland in the autumn of 1969. It turned out to be much more of an ordeal than a pleasure and one in which rugby often jumped from the back to the front pages of newspapers due to the hail of protest, abuse and occasional physical intimidation they faced wherever they went.

With the benefit of hindsight, it could be argued that it might have been better that they had remained at home but the rugby authorities, of whom most would almost certainly be of a politically right-of-centre persuasion, played the dual cards of 'politics not interfering with sport' and that 'more contact brings greater understanding than isolation', and so the tour went ahead.

It will be remembered how London Welsh flanker John Taylor was one of a tiny minority of top players who stood out against the tour and missed out the entire season with Wales as a result. It now seems laughable that on the strength of this he was never invited to play for the Barbarians as their venerable president decided that he must somehow be a communist!

Their first match was to be against Oxford University, which has always been a hotbed of student politics and had to be switched to Twickenham at the last moment. The protests and attendant heavy police security dominated the day and the Tourists seemed sufficiently upset to lose the opening match to a particularly powerful Oxford team led by All Black Chris Laidlaw.

The Springboks had brought the core of the team which had defeated the Lions and were led by their brilliant scrum-half Dawie de Villiers. He had some big names alongside him including the former Rhodes Scholar Tommy Bedford, the athletic lock Frik du Preez, flying wing Syd Nomis and the marauding Namibian flanker Jan Ellis.

Up front John's 'boxing friend' Gys Pitzer returned but injured his back in an early game at Newport and had to return home for treatment. The other hooker was a rather more angular-looking chap with huge sideburns named Don Walton who was thrust into the prime spot. The props once again included those two enormous Blue Bulls 'Mof' Myburgh and Ronnie Potgeiter, a more bony and athletic man called 'Tiny' Neethling and finally the world-class tight-head Hannes Marais. On paper at least they were going to take some beating.

The matches came and went, dominated in the newspapers by violent scenes of running student battles with police and occasionally some overly zealous self-appointed 'stewards' as well. A 'Stop the Tour Campaign' had been launched and was fronted by a dedicated South African activist named Peter Hain who much later became a Labour MP and indeed a cabinet minister. There were co-ordinated sit-downs on the field, nails thrown onto pitches, people chaining themselves to goalposts; it was all a very sad business and did nothing for the reputation of rugby.

Meanwhile players like John Pullin and dozens of others were placed in a 'no-win' situation. No doubt many had deep misgivings about what they had witnessed first hand in South Africa but most, like John, kept their private feelings to themselves and just wanted to play for their country, club or region in the full knowledge that if they declined someone else would immediately step in and take their place, which they might never get back again. Unsurprisingly in the circumstances the Springboks lost several matches they might otherwise have been expected to win.

That autumn John played quite a few more matches for Bristol and also for Gloucestershire who won all of their South West group matches. He played in the first England Trial, which was held at Moseley in November, and this was followed with yet another Barbarians match against an unusually strong Oxford University team. Despite the Baa-Baas having such stars as Barry John, David Duckham and J. P. R. Williams in the backs the Varsity were only overcome narrowly by 18-16.

A week later John was joined in the final Trial by the Cornish loose-head prop Brian 'Stack' Stevens. Like John he was a hard-working farmer who possessed all the natural strength, stamina and hardness that constant heavy manual work would inevitably produce. Stevens had played all his club rugby down at Penzance where the general standard was probably a couple of rungs below that at Bristol but Cornish scrummaging and forward play in general was not for the faint-hearted. He was already in his late twenties, tough as old boots and could look after himself.

For all that he was no giant, being not much bigger than John, and whilst he was not quite in the Tony Horton/Ray McLoughlin class as a destructive scrummager he could be relied upon to hold a scrum at the ideal height for John. In addition, he had loads of stamina, gleaned from countless hours of running on local beaches and could run, handle and tackle much like a modern twenty-first-century prop. He and John struck up a close bond which was to continue for decades long after they had both stopped playing.

The two began their International partnership just before Christmas against those Springboks. Up to that time England had never defeated the Boks in five previous attempts but now there seemed to be a real chance of doing so. The side was led by Bob Hiller and, in addition to Stevens, contained four other men being capped for the first time including both half-backs Roger Shackleton and the future BBC rugby commentator Nigel Starmer-Smith. Also, for the very first time England had a recognised coach in the person of the old Northampton favourite Don White with some assistance from Jeff Butterfield and Don Rutherford who had now been appointed as the first RFU's technical director. Nobody – including Don himself – quite knew what that role actually entailed but he was not allowed any say in team selection.

It turned out to be a fiercely contested match in the deep midwinter gloom and the light was fading fast with the Springboks hanging on grimly to an 8-6 lead as the match entered its final ten minutes. England drove down into a corner and from a resulting line-out the ball went loose and trickled over the line for none other than John Pullin to dive on it to claim the winning try. Referee Kevin Kelleher agreed and then Hiller landed the conversion to complete an 11-8 victory. Whilst it was to be the only try John ever scored for the full England team it was certainly an historic one as it finally broke the seventy-year stranglehold that South Africa had held over England.

On New Year's Eve the Springboks came to Bristol to play a combined Somerset and Gloucestershire team largely comprising Gloucester and Bristol players with a couple from Bath thrown in for good measure. The visitors must have felt a long way from home as it was bitterly cold with a biting crosswind which made for many dropped passes and making goal-kicking particularly difficult. The Boks fielded the same front row as at Twickenham, namely Myburgh, Walton and Marais, while John had the familiar comfort of his Bristol props Bev Dovey and Tony Rogers. The Western Counties pack gained a marginal advantage but the match finished as a rather undistinguished 3-3 draw.

A few weeks into the new year an unchanged England team found themselves under the hammer from a typically rumbustious Irish pack only for Hiller to break their hearts with two sensational drop goals to win the match. Two out of two was an encouraging start and when Wales visited Twickenham a fortnight later it looked like the English might make it a hat-trick as they roared into a 13-3 lead by half-time. The England front row of John plus Stevens and Fairbrother were having the better of it over their opposite numbers Barry Llewellyn, Jeff Young and Denzil Williams and when Gareth Edwards was forced off with an injury, Wales looked to be in dire straits. Just to add to the drama the French referee also had to retire with a pulled muscle but somehow Wales staged a dramatic comeback spearheaded by substitute Ray 'Chico' Hopkins and finally won the day by a 17-13 scoreline.

It had been a case of 'so near but so far' and the England players including John were clearly shattered by having the big prize snatched away from them. To the selectors' credit they for once recognised that a loss against a very good team did not mean that they had to chop out half the team and thus fielded a virtually unchanged fifteen to go up to Murrayfield. They had reason to be confident for whereas the Scots had also overcome the Springboks they had since lost to France, Wales and Ireland and were grimly contemplating a potential whitewash. They had dropped their talismanic captain Jim Telfer with the leadership role passing to John's opposite number Frank Laidlaw, but for once the England scrum creaked badly. Suffice to say Scotland carried the day with a convincing 14-5 victory to send their hordes of supporters home for once blissfully happy.

Meanwhile Gloucestershire had been forging along in the County Championship under the fiery leadership of David Rollitt who was no doubt chomping at the bit at having been overlooked by England. Having easily disposed of Hertfordshire they then won a hard-fought home semi-final against the reigning champions Lancashire. The Red Roses were led by the Mancunian prop Barry Jackson who was soon to win his first England cap coming on as a replacement during the match at Murrayfield – albeit back in the second row.

The Final however produced something of a shock when unfancied Staffordshire took full advantage of playing at home at Burton-on-Trent. Despite a try from John's friend Mike Collins, the accurate kicking of full-back Sam Doble and the plucky display of little scrum-half Jan 'Sprat' Webster (both of whom were soon to play a larger role in John's story) ensured a surprise victory for the Midlanders.

Once again John was away from Bristol over the Easter weekend when he rejoined the Barbarians on an unbeaten tour of South Wales with his England hooking bench reserve Roger Harris also in the party. John appeared first against Cardiff and then against Newport when for the very first time he was given the honour of captaining a major side.

Having held their nerve after the Welsh match the England selectors then wielded the axe with some venom after the defeat at Murrayfield. The big item of news was the dropping of skipper Bob Hiller in favour of Cambridge and Blackheath's Tony Jorden, but dependable lock Mike Davis, Roger Shackleton, Stack Stevens and Bryan West also went out with the wash – all except Stevens forever.

Going to play in Paris in the spring sunshine is usually a daunting prospect and the pack around John included two new caps in Mike Leadbetter and Gerry Redmond plus Barry Jackson at loose-head who had only had around ten minutes' International experience up at Edinburgh. John often felt England could have had a much stronger settled team if only the selectors had showed more consistency. It was to be John's second visit to Paris and it is not a city that is filled with happy memories for him as he was destined to play there for England five times and end up with a record of one narrow loss, three absolute hammerings and a draw.

This was to be one of the hammerings. The French forged ahead and played some exhilarating rugby, which was a joy to watch – unless of course you happened to be English. The rampant French ran in six tries to two and long before the end the England players were chasing shadows as the brilliant midfield of Berot, Lux and Trillo cut loose. Just for good measure they had at last found a decent hooker as well in Rene Benesis. England's season, which had started so well under Don White with the defeat of the Springboks, had now rather fallen apart.

John's own season finished with a return to Edinburgh with an almost British Lions strength Barbarians team to take on exactly the same Scotland team that had overcome England six weeks before. This time the Scots were well beaten with the star Welsh half-backs Edwards and Phil Bennett ruling the roost.

John could now look forward to a rare summer at home on the farm with his growing family – his son Jonathan was born later that year – and take a bit of a rest from rugby. Next season was going to be huge with the Centenary of the Rugby Union and then the glittering prospect of perhaps another Lions tour.

14

Upstairs Downstairs

At a time when England players are each reportedly paid around £25,000 per match on top of salaries of at least a quarter of a million from their clubs, plus any number of commercial deals, it is perhaps worth looking back at the prevailing attitudes of those men who ran the sport of Rugby Union during the lengthy career of John Pullin.

As everyone with even the haziest knowledge of the history of the sport is well aware, rugby football was rent asunder during the latter part of Queen Victoria's reign over the vexed question of players being unable to claim for loss of earnings resulting from their enforced absence from work to play the game. For professional salaried men this presented few problems as they usually received their incomes regardless, but what about a working miner or factory worker who would only get his day's pay if he actually clocked in and worked it?

By the 1890s such men, who largely lived in the North, dominated the selection of the current England team. It is interesting to note that the unbeaten England team of 1892 contained just a couple of players from Blackheath whilst all the others were attached to teams like Wigan, Bradford, Leigh, Swinton, Huddersfield and Oldham.

When the problem became irreconcilable, all those clubs and many others broke away to form what was then called the Northern Union but soon developed into Rugby League with its own rules and the freedom to pay match fees to players. Attendances at Rugby League games invariably far outstripped those at all but Union Internationals and just a few other major fixtures. A similar break was to follow, notably in Australia but also to a certain extent in New Zealand and France.

For their part the Scots, Irish and, perhaps more surprisingly, the Welsh stuck with the amateur code but in doing so the sport of Rugby Union had saddled itself with an image in the general public's mind of being just a bit 'posh'. Indeed, as with so many things in Britain, rugby had somehow unwittingly managed to split itself roughly upon lines determined by social class. This was not universal as, apart from all those miners and steelworkers from the Welsh valleys, farmers from the West Country and the Scots Borders stuck loyally to their Union roots.

For independent farmers like John it was never a question of social standing but any prolonged absence meant somebody else had to milk cows, tend sheep or whatever and moreover usually had to be paid for it. As already mentioned, John was fortunate in that his brothers invariably rallied around and kept things going but for many others it was an insurmountable problem.

The great and the good who administered Rugby Union clung like limpets onto the concept of amateurism with a quasi-religious fervour and seemed totally paranoid about Rugby League. Today a player can flit back and forth between the two codes as and when he pleases but back in the 1960s and 1970s if a man had so much as an unpaid trial with a League club he would be banned from all involvement with Rugby Union for the rest of his life – a social outcast who must never again darken the doors of a rugby club. Human rights? Forget it!

This paranoia about the effect of money was an obsession sometimes carried to the point of self-defeating lunacy. The Five Nations Championship was reduced to Four for fifteen years when France were excluded on rumours of secret payments by certain clubs. For years coaching was frowned upon because it somehow smacked of 'professionalism'; touring teams could not take their own medical staff and best of all Scotland once refused to play the touring All Blacks reputedly because they had numbers on their shirts!

The administrators were invariably ex-players who had grown up in this environment and sought to perpetuate it regardless of social change or indeed progress elsewhere in the general world of sport. Cricket had finally abandoned its frankly insulting 'Gentlemen' and 'Players' ethos by the early 1960s, tennis went 'open' in the 1970s but good old rugby was still trying to perpetuate what was increasingly becoming a tragi-comedy for nearly another twenty years after John had hung up his boots.

Everyone who knew and played with John would testify to his quiet, level-headed demeanour but even today he harbours considerable resentment against the offhand and patronising way that top players of his generation were often treated by those who administered the sport. That great Irish winger and business tycoon Tony O'Reilly christened these grizzled old boys in their blazers as 'Alickadoos' on the basis of their constant chirp of 'All they can do now is blah blah whereas back in my day, etc., etc.'

To be fair many were often very nice people with a genuine love of the game and gave a lot back to it but it was the pervasive hypocrisy and offhand manner with which players were hauled in, cast aside, treated like schoolboys or, worse still, as servants below stairs that stuck in the craw of John and many of his contemporaries.

One of John's England colleagues of the time was lock-forward Peter Larter, who incidentally later became an RFU committee man himself, who recalled,

> After an International match we always had a dinner and dance at one of the top Park Lane hotels. At one point the dinner was male only with the wives of Committee having a separate dining room of their own and then joining their menfolk for the dance. The huge committee of approaching a hundred sozzled old boys and their wives were then all put up free of charge for the night. As for the players' wives they had to make their own eating arrangements before joining the dance and were then somehow expected to find somewhere else to stay for the night. As for the team – they were expected to share a double room with one another. Of course, those of us with wives or girlfriends would somehow get ourselves a room which cost about £7 in the 1960s [probably approaching £200 in today's money] and sort ourselves out. The RFU would then send us the bill and we would all just ignore it.

This pervasive 'men-only' attitude was not restricted just to rugby. When the 1966 football World Cup winners had their post-victory banquet at the Royal Garden Hotel you found Prime Minister Harold Wilson in there bathing in all the reflected glory. However, according to Bobby Moore's widow Tina, the players' wives had to make do with a run-of-the mill coffee shop-type restaurant stuck at the back of the hotel before being summoned back for photos later.

John recalled a similar incident himself several years later when he was England captain and there was a celebratory dinner and this time Brenda was invited as well. It was a pleasant enough evening but, sure enough, he got a bill in the post for Brenda's bed and breakfast. It still makes his blood boil all these years later.

No player at the time expected to be paid a penny for playing and the honour of representing your country was universally accepted as enough in itself. For all that each Union was making comparatively large sums of money for every International match, and whilst the players cheerfully accepted that they were unpaid for playing they invariably felt that they should be treated as adults.

Two England players travelled to Twickenham together on British Rail. One had a cheese roll and the other chose a steak sandwich which was ruled out by some parsimonious bean counter at the RFU as having been 'extravagant'. Perhaps he imagined that biting into a steak sandwich nullified a player's amateur status.

John's friend and loose-head prop Stack Stevens who, as a farmer in the wilds of West Cornwall, had further to travel than anybody else had his own version of a season ticket which was an ordinary second-class return used over and over again. All the railwaymen in Cornwall knew him well, waved him cheerfully aboard and often found him a spare first-class sleeping compartment and of course he could reclaim his modest second-class fare every time. If all else failed he would hitch a ride on a broccoli lorry going up overnight to Covent Garden, which was hardly the ideal way to prepare for international sport.

Even after England's greatest triumph of that era when they beat the All Blacks in Auckland Chris Ralston recalled having to squeeze his 6-foot-6 frame into a miserably uncomfortable economy seat right at the very back of the plane for the entire thirty-hour-plus flight home. Meanwhile the officials could stretch out with their free champagne in First Class up at the front.

And so it went on. As the years went by it all got sillier and sillier until by the 1990s there was talk of players striking and refusing to talk to the media. One famous episode in John's time was the 'saga of the striped boots'. With many years' hindsight it all seems a bit of a lark, which indeed it was, but if highly talented grown men are treated like children what could one expect?

By the early 1970s rugby boots had progressed from the old days of thick leather and nailed-in studs, via rather more malleable Cotton Oxfords with screw-in studs, to lighter, water-resistant items and these often came from Germany. One such firm was Adidas whose

UK representative was an ex-Olympic athlete named John Cooper who approached David Duckham with the offer of supplying free boots with their distinctive three vertical white stripes not only to David himself but to the rest of the team as well. This was eagerly accepted and before long players were going back to their clubs flogging off various Adidas items such as training tops, kit bags and so forth as well as pairs of boots. The RFU officials spluttered into their gin and tonics but again chose to look the other way.

Then it grew. Rivals Gola and Puma, each with their own distinct markings on their boots, got in on the act and before long players were being offered under-the-counter cash to wear a specific brand in televised matches. England's resourceful Number 8, Andy Ripley, famously solved the problem by wearing one manufacturer's boot on his left foot and another brand on his right and thus claiming from both companies!

John had always used Adidas boots and although he never recalled actually getting any money, they designed a particular boot with elongated rubber studs especially for him to use on hard grounds. For some years he had used longer studs on his left boot to get better grip and shorter ones on the other to give himself a tiny advantage when striking for the ball with his freer right foot.

Those payments were all supposed to be very hush-hush but then some of the Welsh squad found out that England players were supposed to be getting more than them and so tried to do likewise. The story goes that unfortunately a certain Welsh prop, who was perhaps not quite as switched on as the merchant banker Ripley, had turned up to play at Murrayfield with boots provided by two different manufacturers but unfortunately had only packed two left ones.

What they would have done with all those luminous yellow and pink affairs we see today God only knows. It had certainly all got a bit Alice in Wonderland but somehow one cannot quite imagine John Pullin prancing around Twickenham in a pair of pink boots!

15

Rugby's Happy Birthday

Back in March 1871 twenty rugby players from England faced twenty more from Scotland at Raeburn Place in Edinburgh in the world's first ever International match. Some 4,000 souls saw the Scots win a lively encounter and it immediately became an annual event which by 1879 was recognised by awarding the Calcutta Cup to the winners.

Rugby had put together a special programme of matches to celebrate the Centenary including an extra England v Scotland match back in Edinburgh on the precise date of 27 March, which happily fell on a Saturday. Other events were a combined team from Wales and England taking on a similar selection from Scotland and Ireland at Twickenham, a short tour by the free-running Fijians and finally a visit from what was essentially a Rest of the World team to make a brief tour of the provinces, including a South West team at Bristol, ending up with a special International match against England at Twickenham.

For the past couple of seasons John's appearances for Bristol had inevitably been spasmodic and several alternative hookers had been tried with varying degrees of success. At last the club had recently found a more than adequate replacement by the name of John White who was inevitably nicknamed 'Chalky' and who conveniently played his county rugby for Somerset. Smaller and possibly not quite as fast a striker as John, he was nevertheless a very fine hooker in his own right and moreover was happy to throw in to line-outs as and when required. In many ways it was a nice problem for the club to have but it was going to create some internal difficulties in due course.

Their hooking styles however were rather different. One man who propped both of them – largely as a loose-head – on many occasions was Mike 'The Greek' Fry. He recalled,

> John would clamp closely onto his loose-head on our put-in and wanted the scrum reasonably high. He was so strong in the neck that he could help me in shoving their tight-head up to just where he wanted him. On their put-in he would often slip his bind on me which of course was illegal so I had to use my right arm to cover his loosened left one in order to hide it from the referee. Chalky however would pull away from his loose-head and was happy to go really low and would then swing at the ball from almost side-on. If it all got too low he was perfectly happy to flick it back with his head.

After a couple of early season matches for Bristol at Cross Keys and Newport John was off on his travels, starting at Lansdowne Road where he played once again for a star-studded Barbarians team in another special fixture against the Centenary-celebrating Dublin Wanderers club. A week later it was back to Twickenham in some rather snazzy special red and white quartered shirts for that combined Anglo-Welsh team match against Scotland and Ireland where he was yet again facing his old adversary Frank Laidlaw. It was an entertaining enough game but one which clearly lacked the intensity of a bona fide International though enlivened by a superb try from winger Keith Fielding.

'Lack of intensity' was a phrase which could certainly not have ever been applied to John's next match against the touring Fijians at Gloucester. The Fijians, with their fine physiques, free running and handling skills, had proved a big hit with the Welsh public six years earlier and the RFU clearly hoped for more of the same. David Rollitt led a Western Counties team and took up the story:

> There were two sides to those Fijians. They clearly wanted to run around and show off all their party tricks but there was a problem. They just couldn't get any usable possession as Watt and Alan Brinn dominated the lineouts and John and his props were doing the same in the scrums. Soon their frustration boiled over, they lost all self-control and suddenly it was complete mayhem.

For his part John describes it as the dirtiest match he has ever taken part in and given some of the brawls he has experienced in New Zealand, South Africa and Australia, not to mention at one or two Welsh clubs, that was certainly saying something! How referee Johnny Johnson failed to send any Fijians off is a mystery as fists, boots, bites, headbutts and vicious head-high and late tackles broke out all over the place.

The casualty list read like something from a war zone. John was led bleeding from the pitch on two separate occasions and finished with fifteen stitches in separate head wounds, centre Jon Gabitass had a fractured cheekbone, prop Tony Rogers was knocked out and concussed, and so it went on. Of course, it wasn't all one way and a few Fijians had to be taken off to be stitched up as well, but as a way of celebrating a Centenary it was an unmitigated disaster. Fortunately, the Fijians went on to show their sunnier side as the tour progressed including a runaway victory over another very strong Barbarians team – another match that John was possibly lucky to miss.

Bristol were only going to see John occasionally on account of all his County and International calls. They were having something of an up and down season although they did have the great satisfaction, despite John again being unavailable, of overcoming mighty Cardiff for the first time in seventeen attempts.

Gloucestershire again wrapped up the South West group and travelled up to Gosforth for their semi-final where they narrowly overcame Northumberland. By this time England had reassembled ready and willing to celebrate their Centenary in style. Sadly, England had by now hit a dreadful run of results which was to yield a paltry one win and a draw from a sequence of twelve matches as the selectors turned one way and another desperately trying to find a winning combination. Somehow through all that chopping and changing John was to not only keep his place but continue to add to his growing reputation and emerge at the end as the new captain of England.

That was looking into the future. In January 1971 the selectors dumped most of the team that had been given the run-around in Paris the previous April and named no less than seven new caps to face a vintage Wales team which at that point could probably have made a plausible case for being the best national team in the world. England's new half-back combination of Jacko Page and Ian Wright, whilst both good players, could hardly be expected to hold a candle to Gareth Edwards and Barry John who were not only two of the finest players in Europe but played for the same club. In addition, they boasted J. P. R. Williams, Gerald Davies, John Bevan,

Mervyn Davies, Delme Thomas and the rest who were all welded together by their highly experienced leader John Dawes. Basically, almost every player in the Wales team had a clear advantage over his opposite number either in ability, experience or indeed both.

John was probably the sole exception and would surely have been the only man who could have slotted comfortably into that Welsh team if only he had been born just the other side of the Severn Bridge. He would have been pleased to see his Bristol colleague Charlie Hannaford get a well-deserved cap at Number 8 from where he had the satisfaction of claiming a debut try. For all that the result was never in serious doubt, although new flanker Tony Neary showed real promise and winger Jeremy Janion missed an easy chance to score just before half-time, which might have dented Welsh confidence had he somehow managed to nail it.

To their credit the selectors did not panic. Bob Hiller was brought back to replace the young Coventry full-back Peter Rossborough who had suffered a torrid time under some of the 'bombs' put up by Barry John and the aggressive Nigel Horton was recalled in place of Rossborough's Coventry colleague Barry Ninnes. The team then travelled to Dublin to claim a welcome if slightly fortuitous victory.

This time John had a clear advantage over Ireland's Ken Kennedy in the set piece and the England backs defended as though their lives depended on it. For all that Ireland scored two tries to England's none but had an awful afternoon with their kicks at goal allowing Bob Hiller to kick three in reply and so squeak a rare but extremely welcome victory.

It was Hiller yet again – the third skipper in as many games – who spared England's blushes when the French came to Twickenham. He was to claim all thirteen points in a 13-13 draw. France had some exciting fast backs on show and had persevered with Rene Benesis, that talented hooker from Narbonne. He had figured in that Paris thrashing the previous April and shown up well and for once John had an opposing French hooker of genuine quality. Interestingly the uninspired hooker from his first encounter with France three years earlier, Yachvili, turned up again at Twickenham but now playing in the back row.

The big games were coming thick and fast and there was the small matter of another County Championship Final, this time against Surrey at Kingsholm who were led by the omnipresent Bob Hiller and boasting an entire London Welsh back row. While the scrums went slightly to John and his front-row colleagues, the Surrey locks Mike Roberts and Alistair McHarg got the better of the line-outs and for the second year running Gloucestershire came up disappointingly short.

England then played Scotland twice on consecutive weekends. The first was something of a thriller, which Scotland won by a single point thanks in part to the unorthodox goal-kicking of their captain and Number 8 Peter Brown, who was the elder brother of the more celebrated Gordon. In those days it was not so unusual for forwards to be entrusted with taking conversions but Brown's method was almost unique. No lengthy ritual of deep breathing, swivelling eyes and yoga-like contemplation for him. He would just make a quick hole in the turf, plonk the ball down, turn his back on it, walk away and then just amble up and hoof it over the crossbar.

More relevant to John was the fact that for the first time he was joined at tight-head by the burly Lancastrian Fran Cotton. By the standards of the time Fran was a huge young lad from near Wigan in the heart of Rugby League territory. In addition to a lantern jaw, which gave him the appearance of a youthful Desperate Dan from the *Dandy* comic, he had a huge barrel chest and back around which John confessed he found it quite difficult to get a perfect bind in the set scrums. Cotton could run and handle better than many and unusually could pack happily on either side of the scrum.

A week later the actual Centenary was celebrated with a return fixture at Murrayfield with both Prince Charles and the prime minister in attendance. The match opened with a disaster when Scotland's centre John Frame pounced on a fumble in the English back line to score after only thirteen seconds. Things hardly improved and England went down rather tamely to lose by a twenty-point margin, conceding five tries to none in the process. With announcements regarding the selection for the British Lions imminent, John was probably secretly relieved that Scotland had called up a reserve hooker called Quintin Dunlop instead of his usual opponent Frank Laidlaw.

As a final act of the season, RFU President Bill Ramsay had assembled a President's XV, which was to all intents and purposes a World XV composed of players from outside the British Isles. They opened a short tour around England at Leicester where they defeated a combined Midlands and South East team that included a fresh-faced young blond hooker by the name of Peter Wheeler. He had arrived at the Tigers the previous season from junior rugby in Kent but following an excellent match against the Barbarians on Boxing Day had made the hooking position his own and was indeed to keep it for the next fifteen years.

Further matches were played and won at Birkenhead and Bristol against regional teams before the final celebration at Twickenham. The President's Team was a virtual 'who's who' of world rugby at the time and was captained by former All Black skipper Brian Lochore while Headingley centre John Spencer led England. This time the Queen herself was in attendance but yet again the English went down – this time by an 11-28 scoreline.

By now John already knew that he was in the British Lions squad due to leave for Australia and New Zealand a few weeks later but would have been intrigued to measure his skills against Australia's Peter Johnson who had by then built up an excellent reputation over several years. He was also pleased to welcome back Stack Stevens at loose-head who had temporarily decamped from Cornwall to the Harlequins in order to try to win back his England place.

The teams lined up as follows:

ENGLAND: Bob Hiller, Jeremy Janion, John Spencer (capt.) David Duckham, Peter Glover, Dick Cowman, Nigel Starmer-Smith, Stack Stevens, John Pullin, Fran Cotton, Peter Larter, Chris Ralston, Roger Creed, Peter Dixon and Tony Neary.

PRESIDENT'S XV: Pierre Villepreux (France), Stephen Knight (Australia), Jo Maso (France), Joggie Jansen (S. Africa), Bryan Williams (N. Zealand), Wayne Cottrell (N. Zealand), Dawie de Villiers (S. Africa), Roydon Prosser (Australia), Peter Johnson (Australia), Hannes Marais (S. Africa), Colin Meads (N. Zealand), Frik du Preez (S. Africa), Ian Kirkpatrick (N. Zealand), Brian Lochore (N. Zealand) (capt.), and Greg Davis (Australia).

Of course, everybody wanted to see Colin Meads although he was by now reaching the end of his extraordinary career, but the three young men who set the place on fire were the Maori wing Bryan Williams, the Springbok centre Jansen and in particular the All Black flanker Ian Kirkpatrick. The paths of John and Kirkpatrick were destined to cross many more times in the near future.

The game over, the dinners devoured and the toasts drunk, it was now time to get down to business and prepare for once again taking on the All Blacks, this time in their own backyard.

16

Lions Unleashed

Any top-quality rugby player from the United Kingdom or Ireland would almost certainly point to a tour with the British Lions as being the absolute zenith of his sporting career. As with John's trip to South Africa three years before, they had usually played sparkling rugby, enjoyed magnificent hospitality and formed a deep bond with their teammates that would endure for the rest of their lives. What they had always failed to do with monotonous regularity was to actually go out and win a series.

Apart from one drawn series in South Africa back in 1955 and a few isolated wins over Australia, the Lions had departed these shores with high hopes only to finish with a familiar tale of 'might have beens', 'if onlys', complaints about biased referees and a lingering sense of frustration and anticlimax. It was a daunting fact that the last time they had actually won a series was against South Africa way back in 1896 and the New Zealanders had never actually lost a series against a side sent out from Great Britain. A few individual Tests had been won here and there but putting a full series win together always seemed to be a bridge too far.

This latest expedition was to be led by an extrovert Scottish doctor named Doug Smith who had himself toured New Zealand with the Lions twenty-one years previously, although he had spent most of the time sidelined by injury. He proved to be a great success, striking a fine balance by taking the social pressure off his players whenever he possibly could and maintaining a level of concentration and self-discipline which had not always been the case during the most recent trip to South Africa.

He was then happy to leave the preparation and tactics to Carwyn James, his brilliant if somewhat enigmatic coach. James was a chain-smoking intellectual with a passion for the Welsh language, its music and poetry and something of a rugby maverick. In many ways he was one of the trailblazers of coaching in Wales with many innovative ideas about how the game should be approached and played. He had only been capped twice by Wales due to the presence of a certain Cliff Morgan but had been a highly creative fly-half for his old club Llanelli in the late 1950s. He had since coached them with considerable success but was destined never to be invited to coach the Wales team itself.

James knew from the outset that he had a glittering array of talent at his disposal behind the scrum. The names of Barry John, Gareth Edwards, Gerald Davies, J. P. R. Williams, Mike Gibson, John Bevan and David Duckham would all find a place in anybody's list of rugby 'greats' and to be the ringmaster of all this exceptional talent he could call upon his experienced captain John Dawes.

Dawes was effectively the 'glue' in the backline who had wonderful hands and timing with a priceless talent for making the other players around him look brilliant. He had led an all-conquering London Welsh team for several seasons when they were arguably (this was many years before the Heineken Cup) the best club team in Europe and as such supplied this particular 1971 squad with no less than seven members.

It was clear that if these stellar Lions backs could somehow stay reasonably injury free and get anything like 50 per cent of the available possession, they could cause the All Blacks some significant problems. Hence the key to eventual success as ever rested with the forwards and it was in this regard that John would have such a vital role to play.

The other hooker was to be Frank Laidlaw – his old adversary from Melrose – who had already been to New Zealand on that disastrous Lions tour in 1966, as had Delme Thomas, Willie John McBride and the outstanding Irish loose-head prop Ray McLoughlin. Furthermore, the two London Welsh back-row men John Taylor and the rangy Mervyn Davies had also recently been to New Zealand with Wales. In other words, there was plenty of shared knowledge about the size of the task ahead. Could they front up to the All Blacks pack and somehow win enough ball for the men outside them to flourish?

When it came to the front row two outstanding props in Barry Llewellyn of Wales and England's Keith Fairbrother were for various reasons unavailable so, apart from Ray McLoughlin, they were all new to the Lions experience. Two Glaswegians had been selected, namely Sandy Carmichael, a powerful tight-head who had already gained over twenty caps for Scotland, and Ian McLauchlan, a squat nugget of a loose-head prop who packed a lot of strength and technique into a body that stood no taller than 5 feet 9 and weighed well under 15 stones. The New Zealanders were to find him a real nightmare to scrum against as the tour wore on. The fourth was a broth of a boy from Dublin named Sean Lynch who had only recently come into the Irish team.

Modern Lions teams take an army of medical staff, specialised coaches, dieticians, PR spin doctors and just about anyone else you could imagine. In those days it was very much a case of 'do it yourself'. The manager, of course, was an experienced doctor and John Williams was in the latter stages of qualifying as one but, as in previous tours, local medical and physio facilities had to be relied upon wherever they travelled.

After the usual pre-tour session at Eastbourne the Lions flew out to Australia where, still suffering severely from jet lag, they fell at the very first hurdle against Queensland at Brisbane. John missed that first match – which was once again probably a blessing – but got his tour underway a few days later alongside McLoughlin and Carmichael against New South Wales on a waterlogged Sydney Cricket Ground. The Lions pack shoved the Aussies all over the park and, despite some more blatantly one-sided refereeing, came through by two tries to none with a final 14-12 scoreline.

At this early stage of the tour the input from Ray McLoughlin with regard to scrummaging in particular and forward play in general was invaluable, especially as the manager, coach and captain were all current or ex-backs. He had always been a highly intelligent student of front-row play and for the first few matches he, Carmichael and John took a series of local packs apart at the seams. John's first match on New Zealand soil was however in concert with Ian McLauchlan and Lynch at Wanganui against an area combination team led by Colin Meads himself. That match was won with something to spare, as were a couple of others, before the first major hurdle, which was the Maoris at Auckland's historic Eden Park.

Hooking that afternoon for the Maoris was the man destined to face John in all four Tests, namely Tane Norton. Again, the Lions prevailed in a somewhat brutal match but it was the next one against Wellington which really made everyone sit up and take notice. John was partnered by McLoughlin and Carmichael and it was one of those rare afternoons when everything comes together as the Lions ran riot to notch up nine unanswered tries and to fall just short of scoring half a century of points.

That night Willie John McBride, who had by then played in no less than nine hard Test matches without ever once being on a winning side, drew deeply on his pipe and declared, 'I really think we have got a chance of winning this.' From that point on he hurled himself into the training with a new sense of commitment and the others immediately followed their talismanic leader.

All sportsmen go through various routines to build up their own self-confidence but they now began to believe deep in their souls that they could actually topple the All Blacks. The New Zealand press and public also began to sit up and take real notice too. Up until then the headlines had been generally a bit disparaging or patronising but now there was a real 'edge' beginning to appear.

Frank Laidlaw was temporarily injured and so John had to do double duty in the 'T & W XV' (another 'Bob Hillerism' for the Tuesdays and Wednesdays midweek team), which meant him appearing in no less than six hard tour games in seventeen days. Then, having comfortably disposed of a local combined team in the small town of Timaru, the party travelled further south to Dunedin to take on Otago for what was to be their hardest match to date but once again secured a hard-won victory.

John was really having to earn his keep and thus turned out for the midweek team at Greymouth against one of the weakest local provincial teams and this time it was a bit of a stroll with winger David Duckham running in six tries. It was an easy game for John as well – the 1971 *Playfair* annual recalling,

> Pullin, at hooker had a field day for strikes against the head and the Lions dominated the line-outs with comparative ease.

All then seemed nice and dandy but just three days later all hell was to break loose.

Christchurch was a beautiful city on the coast of South Island, although at the time of writing it is still recovering painfully from the earthquake that cruelly devastated the place in 2011. The local region of Canterbury houses a sizeable rugby-loving farming community and its team were the proud holders of the country's Ranfurly Shield and as such one of the few remaining provincial teams that could be relied upon to give the Lions a real battle. Furthermore, the First Test back at Dunedin was only a week away and this was going to be the final tuning exercise for the prospective Lions selection for that Test Match.

Nobody knows for certain what was said to the Canterbury team before the match but when they emerged they appeared to set about trying to maim as many of the Lions players as they possibly could prior to the First Test. Fights broke out all over the pitch including an unsavoury punch up between the All Black full-back Fergie McCormick and John Bevan, the Lions' winger. Manager Smith must have thanked his lucky stars that he had decided to pull his star fly-half Barry John out of the firing line before the boxing match began.

Among the forwards it was mayhem. Sandy Carmichael was repeatedly punched and butted in the face by his opposite number Alistair Hopkinson but steadfastly refused on principle to ever retaliate. As the punches kept raining through in the set-scrums John wondered whether his own tour was going to come to a painful end before it had truly begun. Another incident occurred when the aggressive back-row man Alex Wyllie was having an 'exchange of opinions' with Fergus Slattery when Hopkinson sneaked up behind the Irishman and smashed him in the face when the ball was far away, breaking off two of his teeth in the process. The Lions stood their ground and fought back but the collateral damage at the end was colossal. The dressing room after the so-called rugby match looked for all the world like a wartime casualty station.

John deems this to have been the second dirtiest match he ever had the misfortune to play in with only that fiasco with the Fijians being comparable. Carmichael in particular was a pitiful sight with cheekbones and eye sockets so badly cut and smashed that his tour was ended. In addition to refusing to retaliate he had also refused to come off to let one of his less inhibited teammates come on and reply to Mr Hopkinson in like manner. Just as worrying, in landing a haymaker on Wyllie, Ray McLoughlin had contrived to break his thumb and as it turned out he reluctantly joined Carmichael in being ruled out of the rest of the trip.

The Lions had the grim satisfaction of winning the match, generally standing toe to toe with their tormentors, but matters then became really stoked up in the press. The British-based journalists fairly laid into the New Zealanders, especially when the All Black manager, Ivan Vodanovich, unwisely proclaimed that the Lions had caused all the problems by lying on the ball and that if they did so again the First Test would be like 'Passchendaele'. The New Zealand press leaped to their own cause and it all suddenly became a lot less friendly.

John had survived the ordeal battered but unbowed, although the Lions now had to go into a midweek Tuesday match with only two available props who presumably would have to also play in the Test only four days later. He was able to sit out that midweek game at Blenheim, which passed off peacefully, and both props reported fit for Saturday.

Sean Lynch had flown out to New Zealand fully expecting to be just a member of the 'T&W' club but now found himself plunged into the limelight. In any hard-fought Test Match the tight-head prop is a vital position if a team is going to have any chance of winning. He was a tough boy who, unlike Carmichael, would never put up with any nonsense but the fact that he had flown all the way from Britain was a feat in itself for, among other things, Sean had an almost paralysing fear of flying.

Unfortunately for him the Lions repeatedly travelled between venues by air in little twin-engined aircraft and the smaller the plane the worse Sean became. On one flight from Queenstown over the beautiful Milford Sound many of the team got up to take photos and the poor lad had hysterics and punched out a window. For some reason he was also terrified of creepy crawly things, which caused him to be the butt of lots of practical jokes with toy spiders – especially once Stack Stevens had arrived from England to take Carmichael's place.

Ian McLauchlan, despite his lack of size, was a highly skilled prop who liked nothing better than getting his head low under a 6-foot-plus opponent's chest and firing him backwards. As the tour progressed he was to make life for the nearly 19-stone prop Brian 'Jazz' Muller sheer misery. One newspaper quoted an ex-All Black as dismissing him a 'Just a mouse', which was quickly seized on by Doug Smith who referred to him as 'Our Mighty Mouse'. Ian took the intended insult as a badge of honour and duly retained it for the rest of his illustrious career.

For McLauchlan the match at Dunedin was to be a personal triumph as the Lions set the tone for the entire rest of the tour by winning a titanic battle by 9-3 with the only try of the match coming from Ian himself when he followed through and charged down a kick from McCormick to dive over the line to score.

It might be worth recalling the two teams:

NEW ZEALAND: Fergie McCormick, Bruce Hunter, Bryan Williams, Wayne Cottrell, Ken Carrington, Bob Burgess, Sid Going, Richie Guy, Tane Norton, Brian Muller, Colin Meads (capt.), Peter Whiting, Alan McNaughton, Alan Sutherland and Ian Kirkpatrick.

BRITISH LIONS: John Williams, Gerald Davies, John Dawes (capt.), Mike Gibson, John Bevan, Barry John, Gareth Edwards, Ian McLauchlan, John Pullin, Sean Lynch, Delme Thomas, Willie John McBride, Peter Dixon, Mervyn Davies and John Taylor.

The Lions took the spoils but it was a close-run thing. Early on Gareth Edwards had to go off with a recurrence of a hamstring problem, to be replaced by Chico Hopkins. As at Twickenham the year before, Hopkins stepped into the breach and played a blinder but, having fallen behind in the first half, the All Blacks battered the Lions defence for large parts of the second. Tackling themselves to a virtual standstill, they somehow just held out to claim a famous victory.

John and his somewhat cobbled-together front row had more than played their part. His recollection was that the All Blacks had been all over the Lions but somehow had failed to turn their superiority into points.

One up to the Lions but could they now press on and finish the job?

17

Lions Rampant

Looking back on his two Lions tours John reflected that he found the New Zealand one the better in many ways. As a livestock farmer himself he enjoyed visiting a number of sheep farms and exchanging ideas and experiences with like-minded people. Furthermore, there were no language barriers nor lurking political issues and, best of all, it was for once a series the Lions were destined to actually go out and win.

Following on from the debacle at Christchurch, Doug Smith called back to London for two replacements and within a few days London Welsh lock Geoff Evans and John's England colleague Stack Stevens had jetted out to meet up with the touring party at Dunedin. Just four days later John and Stack were packing down together against Southland at the small town of Invercargill in the southernmost tip of the country. The 1966 Lions had opened their ill-fated tour down there and had been well beaten but this time there were to be no slip ups as the Lions dominated not only the scrums but the line-outs as well.

John sat out the next two games but then it was time to turn everyone's full attention to the Second Test back on the battleground of Lancaster Park in Christchurch. With Gareth Edwards just about fit to play only one change was made to the Test team and that was to bring in David Duckham on the wing for John Bevan. The big Welshman had been on fire in the early part of the tour and had notched up a bucket load of tries but this had tailed off slightly and it was felt that the elusiveness of Duckham might prove more of a handful than the more powerful Bevan. For their part the All Blacks replaced the injured Alan Sutherland with Grizz Wyllie in the pack and made a couple more changes in the backs replacing the old pocket battleship McCormick with the slighter but faster Laurie Mains.

A one-eyed Lions fan might suggest that the match turned on a controversial penalty try awarded by the referee against Gerald Davies but in truth the All Black pack with Ian Kirkpatrick repeating the form he had shown a couple of months before at Twickenham won with a bit to spare. The two unchanged front rows battled it out in the wet and muddy conditions with neither side giving anything much away to the other but when the final whistle went the series was all square. That being said the Lions management now felt they knew the answers required to take the series.

John's next match was a week later against Hawkes Bay at the coastal town of Napier and once again there was a fair bit of 'nonsense' with fights breaking out at frequent intervals. In their wisdom - or lack of it - the Lions management had called out not two props but only one preferring to bring out a fifth lock presumably to give the Lions more lineout options. Accordingly, the 6-foot-5 lock Mike Roberts was pressed into service as a tight-head prop with the barely 5-foot-9 'Mighty Mouse' at loose head. By this time the wise counsel of Ray McLoughlin was missing as he was on his way home. Nobody ever bothered to ask John for his opinion but it not only looked faintly ridiculous but it was fairly well guaranteed not to work. It didn't and John was not impressed.

For John it was probably a match he might prefer to forget as he not only had problems in the scrums with his 'odd couple' of props, but he dropped a pass from McLauchlan with the line at his mercy and then got a whack in the eye which led to him being taken off and replaced by Frank Laidlaw. This just goes to show that you sometimes have to take the rough with the smooth. In the final analysis the Lions won the bad-tempered match by a good margin with Edwards and Barry John taking the mickey out of the opposition and a hostile crowd by playing matadors and keepy-ups in the final minutes.

For some reason best known to themselves the Lions management persisted with this McLauchlan-Pullin-Roberts experiment a week later when the Lions returned to Eden Park to face Auckland. There had apparently been some misgivings about Sean Lynch's fitness levels but, if so, why they didn't try Stevens, who was known to be able to play at tight-head if required, remains a mystery.

Auckland boasted New Zealand's second-string hooker Ronnie Urlich and it did not improve John's mood when the luckless

Roberts was forced upright and the Lions scrum shunted yards back off their own ball. Apart from anything else this was grossly unfair on Roberts himself who had played consistently well in his own position. Fortunately, the Lions' superior fitness and teamwork saw them safely through to a 19-12 victory.

There was a welcome week off before the Third Test and the first few days of this was spent at Waitangi in the stunning Bay of Islands. To begin with the weather was vile with a storm some locals reckoned to have reached 100 mph. When it finally relented and there was a chance for some sea fishing, John and his rival Frank Laidlaw joined forces to land a beautiful 14-lb snapper. A perfect day concluded with a 'South Seas Cabaret', which was a sumptuous feast with a rampant lion made of ice as the centrepiece. The players were suitably attired in traditional 'leis' and grass skirts and the evening proved to be one of the highlights of the entire tour.

Then it was back on the plane for 'Windy Wellington' for what would prove to be the crucial match of the series. Just how windy it was can be gauged by the fact that when the plane landed and the passengers were disembarking an air stewardess's wig blew off and skipped away down the tarmac with several gallant Lions in hot pursuit. When at last it was returned to its blushing owner, the doubtless expensive fashion accessory looked more like a rain-sodden squashed cat.

With the series hung at one Test apiece, it was clear that this was going to be the make-or-break match of the entire tour. It was learned that the big lock Peter Whiting was not fit to play and the All Blacks made a crucial decision to recall the old warhorse Brian Lochore to play out of his normal back-row position and put him into the engine room to partner Colin Meads. This proved to be a mistake. Lochore had been a superb Number 8 but now he was not only out of position but was only a shade over 6 feet tall and by then well past his best.

John and the rest of the Lions pack were well up for this one. Playing with the inevitable Wellington wind behind them the Lions forged into a 13-3 lead in the first twenty minutes and although they never added to that for the rest of the game, the All Blacks had only managed one try of their own and 13-3 was indeed how the match was to finish. It was another great day and one that firmly established Barry John in the pantheon of rugby immortals. The Lions had the series in their hands and could not now be overhauled. What they had then to do was to finish the tour unbeaten in all the provincial games (something which no tourists had ever achieved before) and then complete the Final Test with another positive result and thereby clinch the series.

There was another little cameo involving the next internal flight up to Palmerston North for a match with Manawatu and again it involved John's doughty props. John Taylor took up the story:

> Ian McLauchlan was a kindly fellow and had taken pity on the unfortunate Sean Lynch and so had quietly gone off and hired a car to take the two of them up to their next venue thereby saving his co-prop yet another mind-torturing flight. Unfortunately, he had forgotten to tell Sean about this thoughtful gesture and by the time they were about to leave for the airport the lad had swallowed most of a bottle of vodka to settle his nerves and was by then three parts out of his mind. When the Mouse told him not to worry and that they could both go by road Lynch roared back at him 'Oim going wid de fecking lads!' and a ridiculous tug-of-war developed between them. Needless to say, Ian didn't bother next time.

As everyone knows the Lions achieved both of their objectives and before the Final Test back in Auckland they had not only disposed of Manawatu but also North Auckland and finally the Bay of Plenty. By that time, they were all beginning to look and feel a bit jaded. John played in the second match at Okara Park in Whangarei against a North Auckland team which boasted three Going brothers. It was a lively match which the Lions were relieved to have finally won.

And so, to the final climax of the Fourth Test. How different this felt for John than three years earlier in Johannesburg when he had hauled himself off a sickbed to be given a run-around in the last game of a series that was already lost.

It is widely believed that Doug Smith had made a prediction before the tour began that the Lions would win the series as 2-1 winners with one match drawn. If so, he must have had psychic powers for that was precisely what happened.

The match got off to a lively start when Gordon Brown was clouted by the returned Peter Whiting and then – following a badly gashed knee – eventually had to be replaced by Delme Thomas. There was then a lively punch-up with McBride and new flanker Tom Lister being calmed down by, of all people, Colin Meads. This was to be the great All Black's last ever Test, so whether this surprising act of diplomacy was in restitution for past sins or the fact that Meads and McBride had developed a huge mutual respect for one another nobody can be sure.

There was a hoary old story that did the rounds at the time that Brown's knee soon went septic and refused to clear up despite a course of antibiotics. When the wound was properly reinvestigated it was found to contain the broken-off remains of two front teeth deeply embedded in the flesh, thus posing the unanswerable question as to whether somebody had bitten him in the leg or he had booted someone in the mouth.

The match ebbed and flowed as the 60,000 packed into Eden Park shouted themselves hoarse. Mr Pring, the referee who remarkably had handled all four Tests, developed a bit of a problem with Gareth Edwards's put-in to John in the scrum but the honours up front were probably even. The scores were also level at 11-11 with a quarter of an hour to go when John Williams put the Lions ahead again with a huge 45-yard drop goal.

In the last desperate minutes scrum-half Sid Going did a clever dummy run from the back of a scrum just outside the Lions' 25-yard line, thus trapping flanker Peter Dixon offside in the process. Mains slotted the high-pressure kick at goal and the scores were again level – just as Doug Smith had predicted. Both teams hurled themselves at each other in the last desperate moments but then the final whistle went and the Lions had won the series. It was one of those irreplaceable moments in a sportsman's life when all the pain, hard work, disappointments and setbacks just melt away in a spontaneous burst of pure joy and for John and his mates this was just such a day.

Back in Aust Brenda had got up in the middle of the night to listen to the radio bringing the match from the other side of the world. 'I knew John was out there in the thick of it but they hardly ever seemed to mention his name', she complained to a local reporter who had popped in the next day to get her reaction.

The Lions had one hell of a party that night for after all nobody ever goes out to New Zealand and beats them on their home turf more than once. Unless, of course, your name is John Pullin.

18

England Expects

Once again it was back to the farm and family happy but exhausted from the triumph in New Zealand. Perhaps for the first time ever the Lions had returned not only as heroes but some of the players had assumed something of a superstar status which stretched far beyond the normal boundaries of the sport. The likes of Gareth Edwards and Barry John had now found themselves to be as much household names as George Best, Jackie Stewart or Henry Cooper. This was something novel for rugby, exciting but slightly incongruous for what was in many ways the ultimate team game.

Toiling away at the coalface, John Pullin would never have attracted the same 'celeb' treatment but, despite Brenda's initial reaction, he and his Lions colleagues had now ascended to a position of almost universal respect, which was not only far more enduring but would soon stand him in good stead when he was called forward to step up as a leader. The Bristol club paid him the unusual honour of electing him as a vice president while still very much a playing member – something nobody seemed to remember ever happening before.

Once again Bristol and indeed Gloucestershire were not to see much of their returning hooker that autumn – John Thorne actually made a brief comeback to help cover for his absence – and his first run out was in a near-Lions selection for Major Stanley's XV against Oxford University in mid-November.

In the meantime, England had appointed a histrionic Lancastrian coach named John Burgess who had taken an England team – minus all the returning Lions – on a Far East tour encompassing for the first time Japan, Hong Kong, Singapore and – perhaps curiously – Sri Lanka. It was a bit of a mishmash of a team which included a couple of veterans in Budge Rogers and Rod Webb, some current players such as Neary, Starmer-Smith and Cowman and included two new hooking hopefuls in Peter Wheeler and John Gray who was currently studying at Loughborough. All the matches were won but, apart from one uncomfortably close encounter with Japan, the opposition was mediocre and not a huge amount was learned.

Just before Christmas an England Trial was held at Bristol with a further one in the New Year before the England team was selected to take on the all-conquering Welsh at Twickenham. True to selection form, neither Wheeler nor Gray even made the squad for the Five Nations with the dubious honour of sitting on the sidelines as reserve hooker going to a young police officer named Tony Boddy who played his rugby for the Metropolitan Police. At the time police rugby was held in a much higher regard than in today's professional environment but even so it would have been a massive leap up from the sort of fixtures they enjoyed to the International field.

The selected fifteen contained no fewer than six players making their International debuts and were being asked to step up against a settled Wales team boasting ten returning Lions. It was going to be a tall order. On the positive side John was delighted to have in the pack around him not only the durable Stevens but also the big, aggressive Gloucester prop Mike Burton at tight-head.

Burton was all the things that John was not and the two complemented one another admirably. He was a local boy who had been at Kingsholm for a few years and was something of a darling with the devotees of the Shed as very much one of their own. He was a talkative extrovert, occasionally outrageous with a gift for mimicry and the sort of man John could rely upon to look out for him if things ever started to get a bit nasty. If only Mike had been alongside when the Fijians or the wild men of Canterbury had been trying to maim him!

Two other men who were to play a major role in John's story were the bouncy, lion-hearted little Moseley scrum-half Jan Webster and the tall, gangling and somewhat bohemian-looking Andy Ripley. Ironically Ripley, who grew up in Bristol, had never pulled on a Bristol shirt and had only picked up a rugby ball for the first time as an undergraduate student. He had long hair down to his shoulders, wore outrageous t-shirts topped off with John Lennon spectacles perched on a long aquiline nose. He was another total extrovert who hurtled around London on a huge BMW motorbike when he wasn't hurtling around rugby fields like a runaway giraffe in the cause of Rosslyn Park. As such he was another media man's dream.

Nevertheless, John knew that they were going to struggle and, as he looked around the dressing room, he now realised that with twenty caps already to his name he had suddenly become the senior man in the squad. How different from starting out against the same opponents in the corresponding match a mere six years earlier. For all that the English began well and unsettled the Welsh for most of the first half. However, with Edwards and John finally taking charge it all ended rather predictably with a 12-3 win for Wales.

Meanwhile, in John's absence, Gloucestershire had won their South Western group after a play-off with Somerset and had brushed aside Berkshire in a quarter-final. John by then had reclaimed his place from Mike Nicholls and had his new England colleague Burton beside him for a tight semi-final victory over Middlesex at the Richmond Athletic Ground.

The previous week England had given their long-suffering supporters cause for hope against the Irish when they went into the last few minutes with a lead thanks to a try from lock Chris Ralston but then contrived to snatch defeat from the jaws of victory when the veteran Kevin Flynn scuttled over for a try in the last move of the match.

This was duly followed by two more thoroughly depressing resounding defeats in Paris and at Murrayfield despite the fact that for once the selectors had resisted the temptation to chop around a pack which had at least remained competitive in all four matches. If being given a six-try thrashing by a superb French team was not bad enough, being shunted around Murrayfield by a fairly average Scottish pack must have been a sobering experience. It was an embarrassing 'whitewash' and as this was the season when the Irish were in all likelihood denied the Championship because of the cancellation of the Scots and Welsh visits it was a generally miserable year for Home International rugby.

On a happier note Gloucestershire won the County Championship for the first time since way back before the war in a hard-fought Final at Coventry with the team being led by David Watt whose career was entering a golden autumn. This was to see him restored to the England party to South Africa a few weeks later.

On the back of this miserable season prospects for that upcoming trip to the land of the Springboks looked decidedly bleak. The selectors had by then once again dispensed with Bob Hiller and then discovered that Peter Dixon who had led the side in their two latest disasters was unavailable and so – almost as an afterthought – belatedly turned to John. Some might argue that a hooker with his head buried in a scrum was not the ideal position to lead a team, added to which he had never to date led either Bristol or Gloucestershire whilst his quiet demeanour did not fit the stereotype of the fire and brimstone style of leader favoured by many.

Those around him thought differently and would respond in a way few could ever have predicted. Mike Burton took up the story:

It was inevitable that he would become captain at both county and international level. He led by example and he was highly respected by the players around him. He was not a tub thumping swearing blue murder sort of a captain.

He spoke clearly and in a calm and considered way. He asked you to think about what was expected of YOU which always made the lads focus on their particular job. His style was to suggest and not to demand. For example, he suggested that we do not return to the dressing room after the match with any regrets as to something we hadn't done.

He asked that we do the hard things. 'Go down on the loose ball and turn it our way! Be first there and win it for us... If you call for the high ball – TAKE IT!' He would then say 'Lineouts' and nod to Dave Watt as if telling Dave that he was trusted to win the ball but he didn't actually say anything. In that way he gave the player huge confidence.

He knew how to wind me up. He knew I was a confrontational prop. 'Scrums' he would say and he would then look directly at me and tell me how good the bloke against me was and then finish with something like 'Can you manage him?' It was a sort of challenge when the rest of the team were all there listening. I couldn't wait for the game to get started and that was the effect he had on us all.

When John captained England on the 1972 England tour to South Africa and before we played the Springboks at Ellis Park he referred to the power of the Springbok pack when he toured there with the 1968 Lions. He told us they were different men when they pull on a Springbok jersey. He said this a few days before the game in casual talk during the team's leisure time whilst we were sitting around the hotel. In that way he was ever mindful as to the mental fitness required to play at the top level and he wanted his troops prepared both physically and mentally.

In this way he talked about a succession of situations you might find yourself in where your courage came into question.

Remember the Laws were different in those days and the game was much less safe than it is today. Referees were amateur and a high-speed impact could not be avoided by jumping to catch a high ball, you were going to be gang-tackled anyway and if you went down at the feet of the opposing pack you knew you were going to get kicked.

The rucks were designed to get the ball quickly and if there was a player on the floor he often came out of the ruck under the studs of the opposing forwards at the same time as the ball with no sympathy at all from the referee. John kept us brave by mentioning all this in the talk immediately before we went on to the field. My personal view – and other players may take a different view - is that John just said it as it was. He didn't plan every word he said but if he thought it was useful for a player to know something then he would mention it.

In that way he led the England team that went to South Africa in 1972 from the front and we returned home undefeated having beaten the mighty Springboks in front of 80,000 spectators at 6,000 ft above sea level where the lungs burn and the ground is rock hard. Twelve months later he was to lead England to another victory in Auckland against the All Blacks.

Going back to South Africa for a third time John found that the political spotlight on sporting relations with that country had intensified massively at home. Players got repeated requests not to go and there were demonstrations outside their hotel in Petersham whilst some protestors even took to lying down in front of the team bus. For some of the younger players it was all very unsettling but predictably John took it all in his own phlegmatic way.

Of course, John didn't approve of apartheid any more than the next reasonably liberal-minded person but by then he had seen enough of the country first hand to have formed an opinion, which was that the non-white people he saw – and he saw a lot of them – were not necessarily quite as oppressed and miserable as many who had never been near the country would have one believe. Furthermore, this particular tour would break new ground with the England team playing two midweek games against non-white teams. For sure this was still going to be a long way away from the ultimate goal of having mixed-race teams chosen entirely upon merit but it was a small though significant step in the right direction.

The first match against Natal at the Kings Park Stadium in Durban proved to be something of a revelation. The tour was to be crammed into just three weeks with the first ten days comprising four matches which were to be played at sea level to be followed by a further three at altitude up on the Transvaal finishing with a full International in Johannesburg. Natal were led by the ex-Oxford Rhodes scholar Tommy Bedford who had built up a huge reputation in the UK during the past few seasons and had a strong team around him which was confidently expected to win.

The match was played against a provincial team and, as such, did not count as a full 'International', but it was nevertheless the best performance that an England XV had shown for a very long time as John, Stevens and Cotton bullied their larger Natal opponents out of their stride. A 19-0 victory constituted a very encouraging start but they all knew there were far higher mountains yet to climb. Not for the last time did John have to revise his 'graciously losing' England captain's speech to one of the modest victor.

Just three days later he ran out again at the famous Newlands ground in Cape Town. They had read all about the size of the Western Province pack which the local press confidently believed would grind the English upstarts into the turf. For this match Mike Burton had been selected and in his entertaining book *Never Stay Down* he recounted meeting them for the first time:

John Pullin said a few words and we went out into the tunnel. The home side ran past and Stack Stevens and I, the props of the day, looked at each other. Morne du Plessis, the giant number eight went lurching by followed by Immelman and de Villiers, the two huge locks. Stack and I were searching for the numbers one and three on the Western Province backs, so that we could size up our own opposition.

Then the sun set, and darkness fell on the face of the earth – or that is what seemed to happen. Actually, blotting out the light were van Jaarsveldt and Walter Hugo, the Western Province props who were thirty-seven stone and four yards between them. They were monstrous. Stack was not big by some standards but compared with those two he reminded me compellingly of a starving maggot with me as his slightly larger, elder but also starving brother.

As they lumbered past Stack's jaw dropped. 'I don't like the look of yours much mate' he said revealing his considerable ability to crack jokes in terribly unfunny situations.

At times like that years of accumulated experience comes into its own. John knew that if he and his props went really low much of the weight and power from those two monsters would be effectively neutralised. It was to be a very tough afternoon but they came through without mishap and a second, albeit much narrower, win was chalked up.

Between the matches, the practice sessions and similar commitments the team were invited to see something of the country despite the short period of time they were going to be there. At one point they were taken down a deep gold mine and the tour guide switched out all the lights to demonstrate what total darkness actually felt like. They also found out that the Bantu miners who toiled away for hours in that pitch-black underground dungeon were paid the princely sum of one rand per day – then the equivalent of around 50p. They flew over the Great Hole of Kimberley, which was then the largest man-made pit in the world, visited a safari park and an ostrich farm and, whilst in Cape Town, took the cable car up to the top of Table Mountain.

This was a whirlwind tour and certainly not all one of excursions and receptions which merely served to lighten the intensity of their main mission. This was a deadly serious expedition, not only with respect to straining every sinew in trying to overcome the Springboks but, as this was South Africa, the spectre of politics always loomed in the background.

John sat out both of the two matches against non-white teams, which were held in rather primitive stadiums in Cape Town and Port Elizabeth. He left the hooking duties to his deputy, Tony Boddy, while he saved himself for the big match with Northern Transvaal, which was to be held at the towering Loftus Versfeld Stadium in Pretoria.

If the mighty front row at Cape Town which had been so graphically described by Mike Burton was a severe test, Northern Transvaal was the spiritual home of the Afrikaner rugby 'volk' who worshipped their much-loved Blue Bulls with an almost spiritual homage to the mythology and power of the set-scrum. John's old adversary Gys Pitzer had been weaned and hardened in that brutal environment but he had now retired to be replaced by the current Springbok hooker – the splendidly nicknamed 'Piston' Van Wyk.

This game was dubbed by the locals as the extra Test match and it indeed turned out to be the hardest struggle of the entire tour. It was a match in which the English were relieved to scrape a late draw having trailed 3-13 well into the second half. The thin air allowed the ball to travel seemingly miles further than at sea level and, thanks to three huge penalties from the Moseley full-back Sam Doble, they stayed in the hunt. The decisive breakthrough came when Stack Stevens ripped the ball expertly away from a maul and sent out a perfect pass to fashion a rampaging late try from Ripley and a thrilling 13-13 draw was duly secured.

Although the England back row stole the honours, the front trio, which this time included Fran Cotton, had naturally been under massive pressure but had never buckled and at the end came up still smiling for more. As the Bulls had included at least five of the prospective Springbok pack for the match scheduled a week later this draw was, in the overall context, a hugely encouraging result.

As with the Lions in 1968 there was another Players Court for which his farming friend and prop Stack Stevens was elected as a presiding judge. Once appointed, he dispensed merciless justice rather like a latter-day Judge Jeffreys upon his hapless colleagues. Big David Watt was sentenced to be summarily deported for having had an excessive number of medical appointments, centre J. P. A. G. Janion was arraigned for the heinous crime of having far too many names, the future vicar Peter Knight for twice being late for church and fellow prop Fran Cotton for wilfully appearing on a smart golf course in a horrible yellow surfing vest and pair of red carpet slippers.

But now it was time for all thoughts to be turned to the big game at the historic Ellis Park in Johannesburg. That old stadium was totally rebuilt in the 1980s but, back in 1972 it was still comprised of one large but old-fashioned stand running down one touchline with enormous open banks of spectators on the other three sides onto which the 1955 Lions had reportedly attracted a crowd of 100,000 people. All the non-whites were predictably banished to one remote area high up in the gods. Equally predictably they all cheered loudly for England and by the end of the afternoon they would have much to cheer about.

The tour managers Alec Lewis and John Elders, with a bit of prompting from John, named four new caps and John plumped for Burton in front of Cotton for the hotly contested tight-head prop berth. In fact, John made a strong case for Burton. Cotton was still relatively young and inexperienced at this level and as yet not quite the major force he was soon to become when he returned with the Lions two years later. In addition, if the bullets were really going to start flying up front, as he expected they well might, the Kingsholm man was certainly the one he would most want to have in the foxhole beside him.

The backs had really struggled on a couple of occasions and the most experienced centre, John Spencer, appeared to have temporarily lost both form and confidence. Accordingly, the selectors gambled on a centre partnership combining the wiles of Coventry's talented youngster Peter Preece and the direct muscularity of Jeremy Janion whilst switching Peter Knight from full-back to one wing and introducing Bristol's high-scoring Alan Morley onto the other to enable Moseley's Sam Doble to make his debut at full-back.

So John faced his first showdown as the England captain and, as he led his men out onto the Ellis Park turf to face his own career high noon, the teams filed out as follows:

SOUTH AFRICA: Ray Carlson, Sid Nomis, Tonie Roux, Joggie Jansen, Gert Muller, Dawie Snyman, Joggie Viljoen, Sakkie Sauermann, Piston Van Wyk, Niek Bezuidenhout, John Williams, Piet du Plessis, Piet Greyling (capt.), Albie Bates and Jan Ellis.

ENGLAND: Sam Doble, Alan Morley, Peter Preece, Jeremy Janion, Peter Knight, Alan Old, Jan Webster, Stack Stevens, John Pullin (capt.), Mike Burton, Chris Ralston, Peter Larter, John Watkins, Andy Ripley and Tony Neary.

These all rose magnificently to the occasion but the two new sensations of the day were the 6-foot-4-inch full-back Sam Doble with power to burn and a towering kick like a star shell together with Gloucester's hard-grafting flanker John Watkins. Some 80,000 thronged the terraces and the match got off to a stormy start when little Jan Webster was callously kicked and stamped on prompting an early fight. The plucky scrum-half bounced back and led the way to become clearly the man of the match, not least for following up his high kick-through to pick up on the full-back's fumbling error and sending Morley over for the only try of the match.

Early in the match the team were temporarily reduced to fourteen men when John's loose-head Stevens received a sly kick in the head which required some urgent attention and John had to deal with a rampaging Springbok front row for several minutes with a mere 13-stone John Watkins serving as a makeshift prop. Stevens soon returned and quietly 'sorted out' his assailant and it was then back to business.

Unlike at Pretoria, once they had a full scrum, England held the Springboks up front without undue trouble. Despite some harassment from referee Mr Moolman over his hooking positions, John yet again came out on top in the hooking duel. Long before the end, thousands of bitterly disappointed Afrikaners were streaming glumly out of the gates while the English speakers and of course the non-whites cheered themselves hoarse. It was all slightly surreal as England had ripped up the form book to run out as surprisingly decisive 18-9 winners.

The Springboks and their legions of fans were desolate. They then let further criticism rain down upon them by failing to attend the traditional after-match function with their visitors, much to the fury and embarrassment of Dr Danie Craven who had been the paramount figure and spokesman in South African rugby circles for a generation. The press and pundits were a little more gracious and paid tribute to the tenacity of the English players.

For John and his colleagues however it was a deeply satisfying moment. After that dreadful Five Nations whitewash they had somehow bounced back against all the odds, not only to beat the mighty Springboks decisively on their home patch of veldt, but to also go through an entire seven-match tour unbeaten.

It is noteworthy that even to this day no team representing Scotland, Ireland or even Wales has ever managed that particular feat. Furthermore, prior to the match at Twickenham two years earlier, England themselves had never emerged victorious against the mighty men in the dark green jerseys but had now done so twice in successive matches – and as a try scorer in the first and captain in the second John had played a major role in both of them.

The team returned to a champagne reception and soon dispersed to their respective homes. John was now, at the age of thirty-one, approaching the zenith of his career and the next eighteen months were going to prove exacting, exciting and something of a fairy tale.

19

Leading from the Front

The following autumn saw the return of the New Zealand All Blacks for a proper full-length tour of Britain and France. They were still smarting from their recent defeat by the Lions and vowing to gain revenge. A few of their ageing legends such as Meads, Lochore and McCormick had passed gracefully into history but their new skipper and talisman Ian Kirkpatrick had a few genuinely world-class players to draw upon such as Bryan Williams and Sid Going in the backs as well as lock-forward Peter Whiting and John's old hooking adversary Tane Norton. As the tour progressed the feisty little winger Grant Batty, centre Bruce Robertson and full-back Joe Karam were all to stand comparison with any of those who had worn the famous black jersey before them.

And then there was the mysterious Keith Murdoch. He was a huge man with a black Mexican bandit moustache and reputedly a temper to match. The Lions had heard a lot about him when they were in New Zealand but he had never actually materialised. However, when he did appear in the opening match of the tour at Gloucester against the so-called Western Counties (they all came from Gloucestershire) he was to announce himself by giving John what he described as a 'good shoeing' leading to yet a few more stitches.

As captain John found himself opposing their second-choice hooker Ronnie Urlich and, whilst he together with props Mike Burton and Robin Cowling held their own up front, the dam burst behind them with Bryan Williams and company running in no less than seven tries to just a single one in reply from the indefatigable Burton.

Unlike the previous year he had begun his season in early September and was again the captain of Gloucestershire and actually led them in two 'friendlies' against Monmouthshire and Glamorgan, which was something of a novelty in his case. After a few matches for Bristol he had then participated in another of those combined England and Wales teams opposing a similar selection from Scotland and Ireland as part of the celebrations of the Scottish Rugby Union's Centenary just two years after that of England. It was another high-scoring affair which saw the long-awaited emergence of Phil Bennett as the worthy successor to the crown of Barry John who had announced his premature retirement the previous spring.

Gloucestershire only won the South West group after a play-off against Somerset, who were probably still smarting from having not a single player selected against the All Blacks and nearly turned over the apple cart – only losing by 19-22. Just to add to the poignancy the Somerset hooker was none other than John's perennial understudy back at Bristol, John White.

There was also a new competition that had only been introduced the previous season: the RFU Club Championship organised on a knock-out basis, run broadly along the lines of the FA Cup in football. Then Bristol had been knocked out by local rivals Gloucester who had gone on to win the trophy at an almost deserted Twickenham against a depleted Moseley team that played all but the first couple of minutes with only fourteen men. This was because their England lock, Nigel Horton, was sent off for flattening Gloucester's Dick Smith right in front of the referee. It was not an auspicious start for the new competition which was to take some years to really catch on with the rugby-loving public.

This time Bristol reversed things by defeating their local rivals by 16-11 and hence John went into 1973 with not only a potential five internationals to try to win but two major knock-out competitions as well. For a man with both a farm and a young family this was going to take a huge commitment.

When England finally met New Zealand at Twickenham in early January the match turned out to be a bit of a 'damp squib'. The All Blacks played a great deal of eight-man rugby with Sid Going running hither and thither calling all the shots. John was joined in the front row by Orrell's Frank Anderson who came in at short notice for the injured Cotton and battled away manfully. Sadly, a possible try from the young Coventry centre Peter Preece was ruled out for a forward pass and Sam Doble had a rare bad day with his kicking, missing all four attempts at goal. Despite winning 9-0 the All Blacks were heavily criticised in the media for their dour approach.

To be frank they were not popular tourists, had failed to mix well and had lost a few matches they might have been expected to win. Just to add to their woes they had seen their then 'pantomime villain' Murdoch sent home for laying one on a security officer in the Angel Hotel in Cardiff on the very evening after he had scored the winning try against Wales. Although Murdoch already had quite a bit of 'previous' – including telling a venerable Rugby Union official who had innocently enquired if he was enjoying his first visit to Britain to 'F**k off' and 'I don't talk to the press' – John expressed a fair amount of sympathy for Murdoch who sadly vanished again into the backwoods of Australia and was still there when he died in early 2018. 'Quite a few Lions and members of other touring teams got into similar scrapes and it was all sorted out quietly' was his observation.

Cotton was back for the match against Wales in Cardiff but it made little difference as England were well beaten yet again by the settled and supremely confident Welsh. On the way back on the Sunday those two England selectors Alec Lewis and Sandy Sanders called at Tan House Farm. Their question was simple: England were going to send a team to Dublin come what may and would John be prepared to lead them?

Having secured John's assurance that he would indeed do so, they departed to try to secure a team that could somehow compete with an Irish side which had only the previous afternoon come within a whisker of beating the All Blacks. Their tall winger Tom Grace had scored an equalising try with the last move of the match only for McGann's conversion attempt to veer on the wind agonisingly just a fraction wide of the posts, thus robbing them of a historic victory.

This England visit, of course, had been the match with all the security arrangements and was then followed by the dinner at which John was to make his immortal short speech, which is reflected in the title of this book. His Bristol colleague Alan Morley was on the wing that afternoon and made the point that it was typical of the man:

> Despite being quiet, John had a strong sense of his own ability and was obviously a man confident in his own skin. Despite this he had absolutely no big ego. He would sometimes turn up for training in an England shirt and you knew instinctively that

he was never going to bother to try and impress anyone as he never needed to but it was just the first one to fall out of the airing cupboard.

Before all that John had yet another date with destiny – the Barbarians against the All Blacks and THAT try!

The Baa-Baas selected what was essentially the British Lions team of 1971, bringing John Dawes out of semi-retirement. Unfortunately, Barry John had by then completely retired and both Mervyn and Gerald Davies had to stand down due to injury, but it was still a strong selection which lined up as follows.

BARBARIANS: John Williams, David Duckham, John Dawes (capt.), Mike Gibson, John Bevan, Phil Bennett, Gareth Edwards, Ray McLoughlin, John Pullin, Sandy Carmichael, Willie John McBride, Bob Wilkinson, Tom David, Derek Quinnell and Fergus Slattery.

ALL BLACKS: Joe Karam, Bryan Williams, Bruce Robertson, Ian Hurst, Grant Batty, Bob Burgess, Sid Going, Graham Whiting, Ron Urlich, Kent Lambert, Hamish McDonald, Peter Whiting, Ian Kirkpatrick (capt.), Alex Wyllie and Alistair Scown. (Rep. Lindsay Colling for Sid Going.)

Every rugby follower will have seen that amazing opening try a hundred times and it may be worth pointing out that John was the only non-Welshman involved in the move. John throwing into a line-out, a bout of passing, a kick ahead from Bryan Williams which is fielded by Phil Bennett deep in his own half who, having performed a couple of pirouettes of which Rudolf Nureyev would have been proud, sets off a counter-attack passing to J. P. R., who is almost decapitated by Bryan Williams. J. P. R. still manages to hand on to John Pullin steaming up on his left, who in turn sends a perfectly timed pass to John Dawes and from then it goes on to Tom David thundering across the halfway line before hurling out to Derek Quinnell, who in turn fires that flat (would a modern TMO have gone and spoiled it all?) pass to Gareth Edwards streaking down the touchline to hurl himself over the line and send 50,000 roaring fans into seventh heaven. Wonder of wonders it carried on in like vein for the rest of the afternoon.

To their eternal credit the All Blacks threw off all their inhibitions and played their full part before going down by 23-11. Although the Barbarians have thrilled rugby followers all over the world for well over a hundred years, this is still the match that everyone talks about. In January 2018, some forty-five years after the event, all those involved in that move – including John – came together for a special visit to Twickenham to celebrate the occasion.

And so, to Dublin. If the Barbarians match had shown rugby football in all its joyous carefree finery then this trip to Ireland seemingly had the weight of the world on its shoulders. The events of that historic weekend in early February 1973 have already been recounted at the start of this book and how John's opening remarks have also entered into rugby history.

For all that I was myself over in Dublin on a business trip some twenty years later and after a dinner and a couple of Guinness with our local sales manager we found ourselves in the bar of the Greystones Rugby Club. We fell into conversation with some gnarled old ex-second-row forward with cauliflower ears and a bashed-in nose and somehow it got around to that crucial match. 'If your boys had refused to come God knows what would have happened to rugby in Ireland' he said softly. I looked at him and there were tears welling in his eyes and I found myself with a big lump in my throat and having to gaze hard at the floor. Maybe it was that third Guinness but somehow I don't think so.

The merry-go-round continued to spin. Having led Gloucestershire to a narrow one-point victory over a spirited Eastern Counties, John found himself leading his county into yet another Final, this time back on his home turf at Bristol. Their opponents were again Lancashire who were still coached by John Burgess, whose stock had soared once again when he had sent out a North West team which had turned over the All Blacks at – of all places – Workington. His team talks were famous – the very opposite of John's style. He would apparently hammer his fists on the table, kick door frames and even rip his shirt off as he beseeched his men to go out and die for the cause. On that occasion it must have worked as the Lancastrians, who included Fran Cotton, Frank Anderson and the future Scotland hooker Colin Fisher, stole the honours and won by scoring three tries to one in a 17-12 victory.

At last England turned a corner to chalk up two entertaining wins over both France and Scotland at Twickenham, scoring six tries in the process. By this time John at last appeared to have a settled set of forwards around him. His regular front-row colleagues were the ever-reliable Stack Stevens and Fran Cotton, with the line-out specialist Chris Ralston now joined by the dynamic Roger Uttley and finally a highly mobile back row consisting of either

Gloucester's John Watkins or John's Lions colleague Peter Dixon plus the perpetual motion of Tony Neary all topped off by the rampaging Andy Ripley. Things were not quite so settled in the backs but John must have at last felt that he had men around him who could front up with the best.

There was still the matter of that RFU Club Competition and having disposed of the Metropolitan Police on a Sunday afternoon in London they then returned to the capital to win an epic semi-final victory over a star-studded London Welsh who boasted a team dripping with British Lions. If it was not Bristol's finest hour in John's long career with them it must have come pretty close.

The Final against a very powerful Coventry team was unfortunately not such a happy day. Once again Twickenham was sparsely populated as the competition had yet to catch on with the public at large but those that made it hoped to see a highly competitive match. Winger Ken Plummer had been sidelined by injury for a while and his place was filled by Mike Dandy, but nearly everyone else was fit and available, including England's Number 2 hooker John White. This was going to prove to be a cruel irony almost before the match got properly underway. In March the 'powers that be' on the International Board had resisted extending the rule to allow substitutions in matches other than Internationals and Tours and once again the Final was effectively ruined as a direct result.

Within a few seconds of the kick-off John felt his knee give way as he was crashed into by a Coventry forward and went down in agony. There was no way he could continue and thus Bristol had to battle away for the next seventy-nine minutes with only fourteen men knowing that White was writhing in frustration in his seat up in the stands. Prop Mike Fry moved across to take over John's hooking duties with lock Bob Orledge moving up to act as an emergency prop. Fry recalled that Bristol played outstandingly well and he had the immense satisfaction of pinching some scrums off Coventry's England hopeful John Gray, but in the end the odds were too great and Coventry ran out as worthy, if somewhat hollow, winners.

It had been a momentous season in John's career but sadly it was to end on crutches and then in a hospital ward. The only glimmer of optimism was that he now had the whole summer to recover his fitness before a planned England tour to Argentina at the beginning of September.

20

Against All the Odds

The Rugby Union had accepted that invitation from Argentina to make a short tour, although they already knew that it was a politically and economically fragile country to visit at the time. Both Wales and Scotland had visited Buenos Aires over the past few seasons and had found the Pumas to be seriously tough opponents. For all that, with happy memories of the success in South Africa the previous summer, John looked forward to the experience and a series of matches he felt reasonably confident they could win.

An England tour to Latin America was also likely to be intriguing for all those involved. Unfortunately, they never got the chance to find out. Although another eight years were to pass before the Falklands War, yet again politics and civil unrest seemed to be constant companions to John's rugby career. Argentina had been through two *coup d'etats* and no less than five presidents in just a couple of years, the economy was in ruins and brutal riots, shootings and kidnappings had become the order of the day.

The Rugby Union hierarchy received due warning from the Foreign Office that urban guerrillas in Buenos Aires had kidnapped a number of overseas businessmen and other prominent figures and had since made specific threats against the England rugby players. This time the RFU decided discretion was the better part of valour and reluctantly cancelled the tour. Having prepared themselves for the tour the team and management now found themselves with no fixtures.

The New Zealand Rugby Union had been going through some heavy political issues of its own. Their prime minister, Norman Kirk, had ordered the NZRU to withdraw its invitation to South Africa unless the Springboks would accept the principle of selecting its team entirely on merit and with no consideration of a colour bar. Such an agreement was never going to happen and so the tour was abruptly cancelled. So both they and England were all dressed up but with nowhere to go.

With the prospect of an empty calendar, the New Zealanders stepped up at short notice and invited England down for a full international match in Auckland preceded by a short series of provincial matches to become acclimatised. An added bonus would be an extra match against Fiji in the capital city of Suva as a first stop. Early September was not an ideal time for a high-pressure tour and it was all somewhat hurriedly put together but, with the management and team already chosen, all the necessary arrangements were soon sorted out. John now contemplated a return to the country where he had done so well with the Lions two years before.

When the squad was announced one item of interest was that the Bristol club would be providing both hookers. Thanks to John's repeated absences, John White had flourished and was now seen as the heir apparent not only at the club but by then at England level as well. This was no mean feat given the claims of men such as John Gray (Coventry), John Lansbury (Sale), Phil Keith-Roach (Rosslyn Park) and of course the burgeoning talent that was Leicester's Peter Wheeler.

England took only twenty-five players including just the same three established props in Stevens, Burton and Cotton but, apart from a young Cornish flanker named Peter Hendy, almost the entire party had been capped already and fourteen of the team that had defeated Scotland in March were also on the plane. Neither Nigel Horton nor Peter Larter were available and so the extra locks were two ex-Cambridge Blues named Nick Martin and Bob Wilkinson. Bob had excelled for the Barbarians in Cardiff against the All Blacks and was regarded very much like Hendy as one for the future.

The party landed in the burning heat of Suva after a punishing air journey via Los Angeles with all the inevitable effects of tiredness and jet lag. The players were intrigued to discover that among the welcoming party were some of the largest women they had ever set eyes upon. There was a lavish sit-down meal with a local chief soon after they landed and enormous plates of what appeared to be some form of stew were laid out before them. Jet lag had so caught up with John Watkins that he crashed face down right into his plate of stew and promptly fell fast asleep.

Refreshed after a good long rest, the party began their first training session and it was not one they were likely to forget. The recent spell of very hot dry weather had been interrupted by a torrential downpour and suddenly the entire field was covered by hundreds – if not thousands – of large croaking frogs. They were everywhere and players kept treading on them with inevitably gory results and it all became a bit of a farce. John's pal Stack Stevens exacted due revenge on scrum-half Steve Smith by shoving one down the back of his shirt when he wasn't looking. Smith had arrived late for the warm-up, was thus unaware of the frogs and had already gained a reputation for having rather a lot to say for himself. Because of all this, despite his screams of terror – he apparently imagined it was a snake – he got precious little sympathy.

The match in Suva was John's first game back after his knee injury at Twickenham and England only just scraped through to snatch a narrow win by 13-12 thanks to a late try from winger Peter Squires. With painful memories of that awful encounter at Gloucester two years before he was glad to discover that there was to be no repetition of the thuggery that had blighted that previous match. There were some obvious excuses for the tourists' halting display in that many of the players were still jet lagged and the weather was extremely hot – but it was hardly calculated to put the wind up the New Zealanders.

It was then time to move on to Auckland to a less than auspicious welcome as yet again anti-apartheid demonstrators, who if anything were even more vociferous than those back in Britain, picketed them as they arrived at the airport. This had absolutely nothing to do with the current tour but was on the presumption that some of the England team would be expected to tour South Africa with the Lions the following summer. It would have been a reasonable assumption at that point that John would have been one of them and possibly the captain as well.

The first match was played out at New Plymouth in torrents of rain and a sea of mud against the regional team representing Taranaki. John, having got the flight and any rustiness from his injury-enforced lay-off out of his system, gave a superb hooking performance in the mire to take seven scrums against the Taranaki put-in, being ably assisted by Burton and Stevens. Outside the scrum things did not work so well and, having squandered numerous chances, they lost by two penalties to one. Just to add to their woes Nick Martin was rushed off to hospital with what was initially thought to be concussion, went briefly into a coma but happily it then turned out that he was suffering nothing worse than dehydration and low blood pressure.

White took the hooking berth for the second match at Wellington flanked by Cotton and Burton and, although he performed well enough, the England XV went down for the second time and indeed were trailing by 3-21 by half-time. Things improved in the second half but, despite tries from Peter Knight and Chris Ralston, the English could not quite make up the deficit.

The weather continued to be vile and, after missing that second defeat at Wellington, John returned to face Canterbury at Lancaster Park in Christchurch where it will be recalled the Lions front row had been physically beaten up two years before. Some of the old protagonists like McCormick and Wyllie were still there although the notorious Alistair Hopkinson had by then moved on. The match was hard but thankfully once again there was no repeat of the nastiness of the 1971 Lions match.

Although England lost yet again there were very definite signs of improvement, especially in the second half when England scored three excellent tries having trailed 12-0 at the interval. Indeed, only poor goal-kicking prevented them from pulling off an unlikely victory.

Defeated on the day but far from beaten in spirit, John took his troops off to the pleasant seaside resort of Waitangi in the Bay of Islands area to rest and recuperate. This of course was where the Lions had stayed prior to the vital Third Test two years before. Upon arrival and just to cheer everyone up the sun at last came out and some pleasant days fishing and sailing interspersed with training and planning provided just the tonic the team required. Some of the team had been out fishing in the bay and had landed a large and ugly-looking snapper. This was kept fresh in John's en-suite toilet and then found its way into Steve Smith's bed just before he turned in for the night. The resulting scream was well worth all the effort.

A further cause for optimism had been the form shown by the lively scrum-half Jan Webster who had done so much to bring about the victory in Johannesburg the previous year. At Twickenham Sid Going had been allowed to boss matters and had given Webster a difficult afternoon, but plans were now put in place to neutralise the often-brilliant little Maori and Webster's part in this was to prove vital.

The All Blacks had not had an easy time themselves. In their last international match they had lost to France in Paris and their recent Trials had been a bit of a mess. Many of their star names including Kirkpatrick, Bryan Williams, Tane Norton and Grant Batty as well as Going were all ready and waiting but they also included two debutants called Bob Lendrum and Murray Jones in the key full-back and loose-head prop roles with the almost equally untested John Dougan at fly-half. All this gave further cause for hope.

This time the tight-head role went to Cotton rather than Burton and he responded magnificently. The selectors also gave a vote of confidence to Peter Rossborough who had experienced some difficulty with his goal-kicking in the earlier matches but he also came up with the goods when it most mattered.

So, on Saturday 15 September the teams took to the field at Eden Park in Auckland. On their only previous visit some ten years before England had gone down bravely by 21-11 and so the 56,000 spectators settled down confidently in the expectation of a similar outcome. Despite having a couple of relative newcomers in the All Blacks team, nobody expected anything other than a routine victory. John and his men had other ideas and for any loyal followers of England this was probably their finest hour.

The teams lined up as follows:

NEW ZEALAND: Bob Lendrum, Bryan Williams, Ian Hurst, Mike Parkinson, Grant Batty, John Dougan, Sid Going, Murray Jones, Tane Norton, Kent Lambert, Hamish McDonald, Sam Strahan, Ian Kirkpatrick (capt.), Alex Wyllie and Ken Stewart. (Rep. Terry Morrison.)

ENGLAND: Peter Rossborough, Peter Squires, Geoff Evans, Peter Preece, David Duckham, Alan Old, Jan Webster, Stack Stevens, John Pullin (capt.), Fran Cotton, Chris Ralston, Roger Uttley, John Watkins, Andy Ripley and Tony Neary. (Rep. Martin Cooper.)

Things seemed to be going according to the script when Wyllie picked up at the base of a scrum and fed Sid Going who sent Batty zipping across the turf to score. Minutes later Jan Webster (who again was everybody's man of the match) made a crisp break to open up a score for Peter Squires, which was capped off by a fine touchline conversion from Peter Rossborough. The All Blacks then grabbed a second try to lead 10-6 at the interval.

Eight minutes into the second half the two new All Blacks got themselves into a horrible mess. Webster put a searching kick downfield which got fly-half Dougan into a tangle and he then threw a wild pass to debutant Lendrum whose clearance kick was gobbled up by the England pack tearing up behind Stevens as he hurtled upfield. He passed to the long-striding Chris Ralston and then received a perfectly timed return to round the defence and crash over for what turned out to be the critical score. The England pack with John Watkins, Andy Ripley and Tony Neary much to the fore then took a stranglehold on the game despite repeated and desperate attempts by the home team to break through. A few minutes before time the luckless Lendrum made a hash of yet another high ball for the magnificent Webster to set up a further try via Alan Old for the ever-available Neary to put the icing on the cake.

Just to rub it all in the burly Fran Cotton careered upfield in the dying minutes selling two outrageous dummies (one sent the rather morose Sid Going spinning in the wrong direction) before threading a delicate fly-half's kick through the defensive cover, which nearly resulted in yet another. It was just that kind of afternoon.

Predictably the New Zealand press castigated their own team and their selectors but some still found the good grace to praise a very spirited England display. John and the rest of his underrated squad did not care a hoot – this was one hell of a victory.

The Maoris have a haunting melody named '*Po Atarau*', which was adopted to send off ANZAC troops to Europe and to fight and die at Gallipoli in 1915. In recent times it is often sung through misty eyes at the end of rugby tours to New Zealand. It is called 'Now is the Hour' and for John and his players those words surely captured both their performance and that fleeting moment of triumph so far away from home and against all the odds.

21

High Highs and Low Lows

A tour to New Zealand was an unusual way to begin a season. When John had a moment to review his career he realised he had two major bits of unfinished business as far as England was concerned. He had never yet played in an International against Australia nor had he ever been in a team that had managed to beat Wales despite seven attempts to date.

John had not been back in the country for more than a few weeks when the Wallabies came to the UK for a short tour of England and Wales. His experience to date with Australian teams had been limited to a match for the South West nearly seven years before and a game for the Lions against New South Wales in Sydney. In marked contrast to the rather surly All Blacks of the previous autumn they were cheery and approachable but in truth not very strong. They had a few very good players, notably their experienced scrum-half John Hipwell, their hefty lock-forwards Reg Smith and Garrick Fay and an exciting young full-back named Russell Fairfax. Where they were less well catered for however was in the front row and this was to prove something of an Achilles heel.

John led a selection called the 'South and South-West' against them at Bath flanked by his England colleagues Burton and Stevens and a narrow victory was gained in no small part by the goal-kicking of his Bristol colleague Alan Pearn. Three weeks later it was England's turn and they made short work of the Wallabies, winning at something of a canter. Since the retirement of Peter Johnson, they had experimented with several hookers and had brought in Chris Carberry who was a university undergraduate some ten years younger than John. Carberry had already experienced difficulties at Bath and this time he really struggled and was finally replaced midway through the second half.

For England it meant four wins on the bounce and John now held the then unique achievement of a British player captaining his country to victory over all three of the southern hemisphere countries. It was a proud record which he held for almost thirty years until equalled by Martin Johnson long after rugby had turned professional.

Although Bristol were not seeing much of John, he was leading Gloucestershire who topped the South West group once again, although only the boot of the new Gloucester full-back Peter Butler had kept their noses just in front against Cornwall at Camborne.

John did manage a few games for his club around the Christmas period when he faced both Neath at The Gnoll and Llanelli at home. The situation with John White continued with the loyal 'Chalky' covering for John in the great majority of matches. By now he had acted as an unused England replacement, had travelled out to Fiji and New Zealand as his understudy and had recently been honoured by the Barbarians. This was going to become an issue for the club within a few months.

Whilst John had been renowned for being quiet it will be recalled that he was always prepared to fight his corner and had that pronounced stubborn streak. This was now to bring him into conflict with the Gloucestershire committee. Having won their group they went to play a quarter-final against unfancied Buckinghamshire at Aylesbury, which, with the best will in the world, does not feature prominently on the map of English rugby. The selectors had opted for leaving out fly-half Bob Redwood (Bill's brother) for a St Paul's College student named Dave Pointon as well as omitting Alan Brinn and Robin Cowling in the pack for another student named Robert Hughes and bringing in the converted lock Barry Nelmes at loose-head prop.

It may have been that they saw opposition comprised of players from clubs like Marlow, Chiltern and Buckingham as posing little threat and decided to give some experience to a few younger players, but the matter was poorly handled and furthermore the team had stuttered to an unconvincing 10-0 win. Then there was one old hangover from the days of yore which had begun to stick in the craw of not only John but most of his generation of players too. John recalled, 'There was an age-old tradition that the Gloucestershire captain was expected to lead his team in a chorus of "They are jolly good fellows" for the opposition and having not even been consulted on what the Committee had done to the team I just kept quiet and we never sang it.'

Added to this when he stood up to make his captain's speech he was openly critical of the way the selection had been handled. He might have been the toast of Dublin but this latest speech did not go down at all well. Some of the Committee saw this as gross insubordination and muttered about dropping him. Then they came to realise that this was the currently triumphant England captain they were dealing with and any such action on their part would inevitably be all over the press and could make them look pretty silly. It all soon blew over and Brinn, Cowling and Redwood were all back for the semi-final.

The RFU cup once again proved a bit of a banana skin for Bristol who, led by fly-half Tony Nicholls, despite repeating their victory over London Welsh, were to go down rather surprisingly away at Richmond.

What about England? As the New Year had dawned things looked unusually bleak as a new round of strikes led by the mineworkers had resulted in widespread power cuts and the government introducing a three-day working week. By contrast on the England rugby front hopes were sky high on the back of those four consecutive victories and there was by then widespread speculation that John might lead the British Lions tour to South Africa. Virtually all the recent team appeared to be fit and well with the exception of Peter Preece and at last there was a strong thread of experience running through the entire side.

The Five Nations Championship started with a pulsating opening match at Murrayfield in which John again faced his ex-Lions colleagues McLauchlan and Carmichael who propped alongside a new hooker in Gosforth's Duncan Madsen. England first looked like losing the match, then appeared to have won it only to be undone deep into injury time when the experienced David Duckham naively got caught well offside for Andy Irvine to land a touchline penalty to snatch away that elusive fifth win with the last kick of the match. It was a sickening defeat.

The next match was against Ireland at Twickenham on a day when John was to equal the thirty-four England caps record of Budge Rogers whereas his opposing captain McBride was actually surpassing the world record with his 56th, thus overtaking his old rival Colin Meads.

Once again England underperformed and were largely undone by another fine performance from Mike Gibson who scored two tries and generally looked a class above any of the England back line on the day. Although he had by then declared his availability to return to South Africa, the likelihood of John being asked to lead the Lions was beginning to fade. McBride now looked the favourite, especially as his old Ballymena teammate Syd Millar was going out as the official coach.

Added to this John would probably now be potentially under pressure for the Test hooking berth from a tough newcomer onto the scene named Bobby Windsor. He was the first member of the celebrated and widely feared Pontypool Front Row to be selected for Wales and clearly had the same hard edge as John, which would be so necessary when facing the Springboks.

Before the next international a full-strength Gloucestershire team won an outstanding semi-final at Coventry but what was about to unfold on the very next weekend might have rendered everything else totally insignificant.

France had just moved their home fixtures from the crumbling old Stade Colombes out in the suburbs to a freshly rebuilt Parc des Princes near the centre of Paris. It was now a swanky all-seater affair offering superb views from every seat in the near-50,000-capacity stadium.

The night before the match several of the England players spent the evening with John Cooper – the man who was still supplying them with Adidas kit. When it came to the game itself England snatched a 12-12 draw, which, in the light of the thrashings they had been given on their two previous visits to Paris, was looked upon as a cause for celebration. So they all went out on the town to savour the delights of what was then still known as 'Gay Paree'.

Britain was still beset by a seemingly endless series of strikes and now one within BEA meant that all their flights were suspended, thereby leaving the England party, which numbered around seventy people (once all the committee men, their wives and assorted hangers-on were accounted for), potentially stranded at Orly Airport. To these could be added hundreds, if not thousands, of supporters who needed to be back for work on the Monday morning. Ironically it was the sheer size of the group which probably averted the team being directly involved in a major tragedy.

With everybody scrambling around for seats, one of the earlier Sunday morning flights was with Turkish Airlines and the RFU made urgent enquiries to try to get onto it. It so happened that it could only take around half of the sizeable England contingent and so, by some happy miracle, an RFU official made the crucial decision to keep the group all together and opt for a slightly later flight. John's friend Stack Stevens was always under pressure to get back home to his Cornish farm as soon as humanly possible and had therefore arranged to be woken up to try for an early flight. By a happy stroke of fate, the effects of the previous evening's revelry made him sleep through his alarm call and so he had no option other than to come back along with everyone else.

Later that morning they all flew uneventfully back to Heathrow on a Pakistani Airlines jet to be met at the barrier by an ashen-faced RFU official who just croaked to them all 'Please everybody phone home immediately.' Everyone was still oblivious to the fact that the earlier Turkish Airlines Flight 981 from Orly to London had crashed just a few minutes after take-off killing every single one of the 346 people on board. Among the dead was the players' friend John Cooper.

As so often happens, instant newsflashes can be cruelly misleading and, to make matters worse, one report had mentioned 'a rugby team'. Back home in Aust Brenda was fortunately blissfully unaware of the unfolding drama and was thus spared an hour of mental torture which had affected many of the players' wives and families. English rugby had somehow narrowly avoided its own version of the Munich Air Disaster.

Gloucestershire then travelled up to Merseyside to regain the County Championship at Blundellsands against a Lancashire team now led by John's England colleague Tony Neary. Two tries from Alan Morley and some more accurate goal-kicking from Peter Butler saw them safely through by 22-12.

From near tragedy the England team was to bounce back again a fortnight later to claim that elusive victory over Wales with a particularly energetic performance by the pack. In doing so John was at last able to state categorically that he had appeared in winning England teams against every single International Board nation. This victory might yet have earned him a place on the plane to South Africa but for once the England front row lost the scrum count by 2-5 and this might just have finally counted against him.

When the Lions tour party was named shortly afterwards as far as John was concerned it proved to be a major disappointment. The selectors had not only named Bobby Windsor but had reverted to Ireland's Ken Kennedy to fill the other hooking berth. Kennedy had toured once before way back in 1966 on the disastrous Lions tour of New Zealand but had not featured since. Fergus Slattery, who was a key member of both the 1971 and 1974 Lions teams, remarked that he felt John's solidity and total commitment should have given him at least a place in the party even if Windsor might possibly have claimed the Test position. For all that it was going to prove to be a particularly powerful squad that ran through South Africa like a bush fire winning every single match right up to the last when – as in 1971 – they had to content themselves with a draw.

Before the Lions left John took part in two special matches to raise funds for the widows and families of the players from Bury St Edmunds who had been the unfortunate rugby team to have featured in those early and misleading newsflashes from Paris. John turned out at Bedford for an invitation team called the Bosuns against a 'Midland Counties' team that included Peter Wheeler, and then rounded things off when he led an England XV against a France XV in an extra, rather downbeat, 'unofficial' match at Twickenham. In fact, the most noteworthy incident was the appearance of a long-haired male streaker prancing up the touchline before having his 'crown jewels' discreetly covered up by a policeman's helmet.

If ever there was a season of ups and downs then 1973/74 surely was just that.

22

Pullin or Wheeler and Trouble Down Under

John's non-selection for the 1974 Lions tour was something of a shock not only to the man himself but to many in the rugby press and public at large. The current England pack was clearly highly regarded and all three of his recent props had been invited. (Stack Stevens had to reluctantly decline because of farming commitments but Cotton and Burton were safely on the plane to South Africa.) Added to them both second rows Ralston and Uttley, plus two back-row men, Neary and Ripley, had all been duly selected and yet curiously their undisputed leader had not.

If that was not enough, he now found himself in the middle of another controversy of which he may have been the cause but was certainly not of his making. During his prolonged absences from the Bristol club on county and international business Chalky White had not only acted as a first-class deputy but had also become a highly respected member of the club and was the established captain of Somerset. With this in mind the players (who traditionally elected their own captain each season) nominated Chalky to be their next skipper. The Bristol committee members were of the opinion that this would create an embarrassing situation as and when the name of John Pullin was available to appear on the team sheet. Would the elected captain have to stand down (and to his eternal credit White had repeatedly done so for several years without demur) or would the current captain of England have to turn out for Bristol's second team?

What worried them even more was the prospect of their star player decamping to Gloucester (their keenest local rivals) where he would undoubtedly have been welcomed with open arms. For his part John had never hidden his affection for playing at Kingsholm, which was a much more 'edgy' environment than the old Memorial

Ground could ever be. When pressed as to whether he would have actually made the move he confirmed that if playing second-team rugby endangered his England place then he would not have hesitated in doing so. The Committee then suggested that White's appointment might be deferred for a year although it seemed quite likely that the same situation might well recur once again.

In the end White sportingly decided to turn down the appointment and the honour passed to utility-back David Tyler and the situation was thus resolved. This was just as well as John was to be available more frequently for his club in the forthcoming season than he had been for some considerable time. This was in no small way due to the fact that although John was still to be very much in the frame as far as England were concerned, the Gloucestershire team was to feature the Moseley hooker David Protherough as it retained the County Championship.

The Lions had returned triumphantly from South Africa where Bobby Windsor had claimed the Test hooking position in a pack which, perhaps for the first time, was just as big and as mean as the Springboks themselves, and with Kennedy staying fit and well there was no late call for John to come out and join them. John's Bristol teammate Alan Morley joined the second half of the tour as a replacement but was only to feature in two provincial matches.

With no major tours to the UK planned, England faced the new season with the prospect of only four matches, although one would involve another trip back to Dublin. The 'troubles' had continued unabated and indiscriminate bombing had even begun to spread to England. On a more cheerful note Wales and Scotland had resumed playing in Dublin without any problems and so this time there was little prospect that England would not continue to do likewise.

When the Area Trials came around in December he led the South West against the London area on Rosslyn Park's ground but then found for the first time in several years that he had a serious rival for his England place. When the teams were announced for the England XV versus The Rest match just prior to Christmas, John found himself in 'The Rest XV' opposing Leicester's Peter Wheeler in the 'England' one. He now realised that he would have a real battle on his hands if he was to retain his place.

Wheeler recounted his rivalry with John:

Of course, I had a huge respect for his skills both as a hooker and as a leader but oddly we never toured together nor – apart from those England trials – did we meet very much in opposition.

Leicester used to play Bristol twice a season but the fixtures were traditionally just before Christmas when the England trials were on and then over Easter when one or other of us always seemed to be away in Wales with the Barbarians. When we did actually meet he was a real handful as his legs would be all over you and I knew I needed to be bound extra tight to my loose-head to stop him coming across and blocking my heel.

With the benefit of hindsight, it can be safely stated that both men were truly world-class players but were very different despite playing in the same position. Several contemporaries of both men remarked that John was the physically stronger and faster hooker in a set-scrum (which of course was the bread and butter of his job) but that Wheeler would frequently display a broader range of rugby skills. He welcomed the chance to throw into line-outs, would be seen popping up with ball in hand rather more frequently and scored quite a few tries every season. He even had a spell as Leicester's front-line goal-kicker and actually kicked three conversions for an England XV in Tokyo when still a fresh-faced youth.

John was thirty-three by now, which many would argue was when a hooker was in his prime, but one had to balance that against all the hard matches at home and abroad he had come through, not to mention the never-ending demands of farm work and a young family. Many distinguished players might have called it a day or just played a bit of club rugby for fun but that old competitive streak was never going to let him relinquish his England place without a fight.

The day after Boxing Day he captained the Barbarians to a thumping 43-4 thrashing of Leicester whose hooker and captain that day was none other than the self-same young Mr Wheeler. It turned out to be the last occasion John represented the Barbarians as a player but there can hardly ever have been a sweeter one.

When the team for the trip to Dublin was announced John found that he had indeed been preferred to Wheeler but this time would travel only as a player and that the captaincy had been handed to Lancashire's Fran Cotton who was due to cross over to loose-head in the place of the thirty-five-year-old Stack Stevens with Mike Burton back at tight-head.

The RFU had turned once more back to the fire and brimstone approach of John Burgess as coach and as a man who had been doing the job for Lancashire and the North West he clearly favoured one of his own. To date Cotton had played all his International rugby as a tight-head and had continued to do so with conspicuous success with the Lions the previous summer. He was clearly by now a magnificent player but asking a man to lead his country for the first time out of his normal position seemed a curious decision.

As it happened Mike Burton promptly got himself, possibly harshly, sent off playing in a County quarter-final at Bristol and then unwisely compounded his problems by bowing mockingly to the assembled committeemen in the stand. Accordingly, he was 'withdrawn' from the team to travel to Ireland for Stevens to be reinstated with Cotton to revert back to his more familiar tight-head role.

England did rather better than the previous three fixtures against the Irish and might have stolen a win until a mix-up behind the scrum after John had struck cleanly resulted in a try for fly-half Billy McCombe. Ireland's new hooker Pat Whelan, with the wily veteran Ray McLoughlin at his side, reportedly did quite well against John and so the 'Pullin or Wheeler' question was being posed once more.

When the team was announced to face France two weeks later it was Wheeler who was given the nod by Burgess and John thus found himself back on the replacements' bench – a situation he had not found himself in since 1967 when they were still acting merely as 'travelling reserves'. One improvement since those days was the fact that at least a replacement now had a slim chance of getting involved if one of the team sustained an injury serious enough to be taken off. He was far from the only selection casualty as Peter Dixon, Alan Old and a newcomer called Bill Beaumont (who had only been brought in when Roger Uttley pulled out with an injury) all were given the chop as well. Nobody at that time could possibly have predicted that Beaumont would rise to the eminence in the sport that he was to assume over the next few years.

France had made many more changes than England but hit form on the day and ran their hosts ragged, scoring no less than four tries into the bargain. Wheeler kept his place for the visit to Cardiff to face a Wales team which now featured the entire famous Pontypool Front Row so beloved by Max Boyce and a generation of Welshmen. Just after half-time Wheeler's neck gave way and he had to go off, by which time Wales were well in front and cruising. John came on and things began to improve until five minutes before the end the big policeman Nigel Horton crashed over the line to register England's only points. This only served to wake the Welsh up again and they came back to get a final try from centre Steve Fenwick. The era of Burgess and Cotton had so far yielded a depressing series of three defeats and having conceded nine tries in the process.

Burgess and the selectors really thrashed around for the visit of the Scots to Twickenham. With Wheeler nursing his neck injury, John retained his place and was rejoined by Mike Burton who was clearly deemed to have now made amends for his faux pas at Bristol. They also recalled Andy Ripley, who had been mysteriously omitted in Cardiff, and then surprisingly recalled scrum-half Jacko Page who had not featured since 1971 and, even more sensationally, Dave Rollitt who had been completely out of favour for no less than six years. Alan Morley, a third Bristol man, was also brought back and scored the only try of a dreary match in which England squeaked home by a 7-6 scoreline.

John found himself back on the bench again for Irelands' Centenary match in Dublin when he was covering for Bobby Windsor in yet another of those combined England and Wales matches against the Scots and Irish.

To say that English selectors over the years were capricious would be to put it politely. Next on the agenda was a medium-length tour of Australia and they seemed to have convinced themselves that the Wallabies would be easy prey based upon their previous season's mediocre performances in the UK. Accordingly, they decided it would be an ideal opportunity to 'blood' a few new faces. Just how bloody some of those faces would become soon became apparent!

Whilst it is usually a good plan to give one or two newcomers an opportunity alongside an experienced core, this time a whole parade of 'wannabees' was included – many of whom were to sink and disappear almost without trace. With Cotton absent for the Scotland match, the captaincy had been passed by Burgess, not back to John but to another of his Lancastrian henchmen, Tony Neary, who was now going to be asked to continue the role despite Cotton's return as a player.

Seemingly half a generation of recent England players were summarily axed including Ralston (who had been in a Lions Test only nine months before), Stevens, Rossborough, Webster,

Old, Smith, Dixon and Cooper, not to mention Robin Cowling who had sat impatiently on the bench as the heir apparent prop all season.

When John met up with the rest of the touring party there were a whole lot of faces he would barely have recognised. Meanwhile Peter Wheeler had only just begun playing again and was unavailable to go. This situation was hardly fair on the new men, which included John Raphael (the other hooker), future England coach Brian Ashton, Neil Mantell, Steve Callum, Ian Orum, Alan Wordsworth and Derek Wyatt, none of whom were ever to get the chance to show what they might potentially have produced. For some time, it seemed that Gloucester's highly promising prop Phil Blakeway might have suffered the same fate before he finally broke back into the reckoning a full five years later.

Apart from John, the experienced forwards remaining in the party were Neary, Cotton, Burton, Uttley and Ripley, to which could be added Dave Rollitt, who had seemingly returned to favour after spending six of the best years of his career in the International wilderness. He had always been a plain-speaking Yorkshireman and it was muttered that he had 'said his piece' rather too pungently to some of his teammates who had more or less run up the white flag down in Cardiff some years before and had upset one two sensitive souls in the RFU in the process. There were quite a few times when his rugby brain and iron will might have helped England's cause at crucial moments.

In his *Book of English International Rugby* author John Griffiths dismisses the entire adventure with the harsh words 'England's short tour of Australia was an unmitigated failure.' Manager Alec Lewis and John Burgess must have felt they had both walked under ladders given the run of bad luck they seemed to encounter at every turn.

Alan Morley recounted how the general atmosphere was unusually antagonistic off the pitch as well as on it. Cricketers are quite accustomed to all the usual 'Pommy B*****d' nonsense, which is ostensibly only laddish banter but can still get pretty tedious after a while, and there was very much an edge to the general atmosphere.

If the Wallabies' poor results in Britain the previous year had led the English to underestimate them, the Australians, no doubt reflecting their general resentment, appeared to want to start fights seemingly without any provocation. Having taken part in a routine early win against a very modest Western Australia team in Perth, John had to sit and watch the team go down to a team representing Sydney in the second match in which Fran Cotton suffered a debilitating back injury that ruled him out for the rest of the tour. For this match the Australians had selected – and continued to select – a malicious prop who took it upon himself to slyly punch everyone in sight without any apparent rhyme or reason. The various local referees each seemed to turn a blind eye to all of this and the atmosphere rapidly degenerated from bad to worse.

John was back for the next game against New South Wales when a close match was won largely thanks to four tries from Coventry's talented Peter Preece. Yet another midweek game was lost at the small town of Goulburn before John returned for the first of two Tests which was played back at the famous old Sydney Cricket Ground. It was one of those days when just about everything that could go wrong found a way of doing so. England's best three-quarter Preece failed a fitness test and had to be withdrawn and within twenty minutes England had lost not only fly-half Neil Bennett but – worst of all – the tour captain Tony Neary who also suffered a back injury to rule him out of the rest of the tour.

John was already having to cope with having a debutant playing at loose-head in the ample person of Barry Nelmes. Of course, he knew Barry well enough from his Bristol days, although at that time he had been a lock-forward but had recently converted to prop after transferring his allegiance to Cardiff. Now at yet another crisis point he became, by default, the captain of England once more.

It was by then probably already a bit of a lost cause. That 'phantom puncher' (who was publicly identified in the press as a man called Steve Finnane) continued where he had left off a week earlier and there was also a highly mobile but particularly wild individual in their back row named Ray Price. Needless to say, there was at least one almighty punch-up, which did little to improve matters, and though England predictably lost, it was only by a 9-16 scoreline with the teams registering one try apiece.

There was still plenty of rancour in the air when John led out England on the following Saturday at Brisbane for a match that became infamous as the 'Battle of Ballymore'. The Australians had appointed a local Brisbane referee named Bob Burnett and probably the kindest thing that could be said about him was that he was hopelessly out of his depth to deal with what would immediately unfold before him.

The Wallabies kicked off and England fielded the ball. A ruck formed and the Wallaby pack hurled themselves in, kicking everybody in sight and particularly poor Barry Nelmes who lay helplessly trapped on the ground as Wallaby prop Stuart McDougall booted him mercilessly like a rag doll. All this was seen as clear as daylight on television. The feeble referee however did absolutely nothing and the ball went into touch. At the ensuing line-out every England forward belted his opposite number and utter mayhem broke out. When it had at last died down the referee warned Mike Burton for planting what he calls a 'Kingsholm kiss' on the face of the self-same Mr McDougall.

A few moments after things had at last appeared to have simmered down the ball was kicked clear and, following up, Burton late-tackled an Australian wing and was promptly sent off by the now panicky Mr Burnett. Burton was nobody's angel and never pretended otherwise but if only the referee had dealt properly with that unprovoked outbreak of violence right at the kick-off things might have been quite different.

As captain a mass of thoughts rushed through John's mind. His first instinct was to lead his men off the field and thus bring the match to a sensational end. There was uproar all around; he had nobody to turn to but he knew full well that there would be one hell of a row back at Twickenham and he would in all probability have been 'hung out to dry' by the authorities. On the other hand, the referee had completely 'lost it' and if this was all going to be allowed to carry on somebody was likely to get seriously hurt.

His years of accumulated experience told him that if a man had been sent off it often calmed things down, although he now faced the grim prospect of playing another seventy-five minutes of a Test Match with only seven forwards including one converted lock as one prop – Barry Nelmes – and a makeshift prop pushed up reluctantly from the second row. In the event Bill Beaumont stepped up, had his eye badly cut from yet another cheap shot but stuck it out manfully to enhance his growing reputation.

Thus John decided not to turn his sense of outrage both at the initial assaults and that of the injustice to his friend Mike Burton into leading his men off the pitch and thus did not provoke what would undoubtedly have become a major sporting diplomatic incident. Fortunately, the match was completed but with England again losing – this time conceding five tries in the process. Ironically when the Wallabies stopped trying to maim people and actually began to run with the ball they began to look like quite a good team.

There was a predictable outcry in the press about all the rough stuff and there were even some dark mutterings about withdrawing the invitation to Australia to embark on a long tour of the UK the following winter. Once tempers had cooled down a bit the Wallaby tour of 1975–76 was confirmed and passed off without undue problems.

Although he did not know it for certain he suspected that his reign as England's captain had come to a rather dispiriting end. After the triumphs in Johannesburg and Auckland it was a shame it was to end with this squalid affair in Brisbane.

23

Not Quite a Veteran

The career of a top rugby player at that time rarely lasted much longer than a decade even if he had been lucky with regards to injuries and had an understanding wife. The demands of following a career and its impact not only upon availability for matches but the sheer grind of training several times a week and the lengthening of the time required to shake off all the usual bumps, twists and bruises inevitably took its toll and even in the forwards only very few were still being selected at the highest levels beyond the age of thirty-two.

John on the other hand was far from finished and was to have another three years before he was eventually to call it a day. If anything, the pace was briefly to quicken even further. He had barely arrived back to the farm and unpacked his suitcases before he was flying off again – this time back to Canada with Bristol.

This was an ambitious undertaking for a club team that was made up of three long-standing 'near-veterans' in Watt, Rollitt and John who were returning to Canada some eight years after their initial foray with England back in 1967. They were joined by a clutch of experienced men including Mike Fry, Ken Plummer, Dave Tyler, Andy Munden, Alan Pearn and Chalky White whilst most of the rest of the party were all still at an early stage in their careers.

The tour was to feature five matches all in the Eastern side of the huge country and would involve individual matches in Montreal, Ottawa and London (Ontario) before finishing with two more in Toronto before flying home. As it took place in August the weather was predictably hot although thankfully all the games were scheduled to have 6 p.m. kick-off times.

It was the first time that the Bristol club had undertaken a long-distance tour as the furthest they had ventured to date had been to Clermont Ferrand for a two-match trip several years earlier, which John recalls as involving more fighting than actual rugby. Club rugby in France in those days was not for the squeamish.

Despite the fact that Bristol managed to win every game, all their matches were of a reasonable standard and, apart from the opening game, were fairly competitive with the final match only being won by 12-6. To save on costs the players were all hosted in local rugby supporters' houses. In the small city of London, it transpired that John, Rollitt and Watt were the guests of a hospitable man named Jeff Chambers. He and the players had returned to the house one evening and Chambers had driven off to a nearby convenience store to pick up some more beer. Standing around outside John peered through the windows and tried the doors to see if they could somehow get in to wait for him. A zealous neighbour spotted them and immediately called the police. The next thing John knew was that he was facing a large fat cop pointing a gun at him, spread-eagling him over the bonnet of a parked car and then attempting to kick his legs away. Fortunately, the host returned and all was sorted out amicably. John would happily face down an irate 20-stone Transvaal prop but being threatened with a loaded gun was not an experience he was anxious to repeat.

September 1975 found him back with Bristol and towards the end of the month he led a President's XV, largely made up of current England players, against a Somerset team led by John White. This was followed by appearing in all the South West group county matches and he then captained the Western Counties in a midweek floodlit match on the Memorial Ground with the Wallabies.

He knew full well that his England place was now under intense pressure from the competing claims of Peter Wheeler and played against him in no less than three England Trials. These took on a slightly different format when John travelled to Wheeler's home patch at Welford Road in Leicester to hook for an England XV against a team drawn from the 'North and Midlands' who won the match by 18-10. John recalls this as a key point in finally losing his place to Wheeler. The North/Midlands team had a new tight-head prop called Will Dickinson who plied his trade for Richmond. He scrummaged extremely low against the taller Barry Nelmes and thus gave John all sorts of problems, which of course worked very much to Wheeler's benefit.

A week later the situation was reversed at Gloucester with Wheeler in the England XV and John captaining the South. A few days before Christmas the final showdown took place at Twickenham with Wheeler now embedded in the 'England XV' alongside Cotton and Burton whilst John now found himself in the 'Rest' team partnered by Barry Nelmes and the Wasps tight-head prop Brian Adam. Selectors being what they are ensured that the unlucky Dickinson was now nowhere to be seen. This time there were no upsets with the likely England team comfortably winning by a 39-21 scoreline notching four tries to one in the process.

Thus, John was to find himself back sitting on the sidelines whilst England gained sweet revenge over their Brisbane tormentors from Australia and watching Wheeler winning the scrums 4-0 as he settled into the position. This situation was to continue throughout the season as John was forced to sit in the wings as England went on to lose every single Five Nations match to finish bottom of the table once again for the fourth time in five years.

In fact, there was to be one more twist in the tale. Having already lost all their previous three games England were due to fly out to Paris for the final match very much on a hiding to nothing. After yet another defeat at Murrayfield the selectors had turned away from some of their most experienced men in Duckham, Old and Ripley and once again sent something of a cobbled-together team to attempt to take on a powerful French team who had at last settled upon a really powerful front row of Gerard Cholley, Alain Paco and Robert Paparemborde. At the very last minute, Wheeler had to withdraw with an injury that had not cleared up as expected after having already missed the pre-match run-out back in London while he was frantically trying to find his missing passport! Accordingly, and for the very last time, John pulled on the white England Number 2 shirt and went out once more to do battle.

If he had any nightmares about the chasings he had endured from the French on a spring afternoon in Paris from 1970 and 1972, not to mention the narrow squeak with the Turkish Airlines crash a mere two years before, they must have all come racing back. To put it bluntly, England never looked like having a chance and were put to the sword by a rampant French team that ran in six tries to one solitary effort by a gallant Peter Dixon – another returning prodigal son who had been ignored for the past eighteen months.

John thus finished his distinguished England career on a slightly sombre note. He had by then amassed more England appearances – forty-two – than any other man in the history of the sport and had the unique honour of leading his country to victory against all the three southern hemisphere countries. Had this all taken place in the modern professional era with often ten or twelve International matches taking place in a single season (not to mention replacements running on whenever someone begins to look a bit tired or at the sight of a bang on the head or a nosebleed) then this total would certainly have been up there over the century mark with the Jason Leonards of this world.

He was now in his thirty-fifth year with an elderly father plus a wife and two children at home, but he was still fit as ever and had certainly not reached the stage when he could be classed as a veteran. But still the big matches and overseas tours continued to arrive thick and fast.

Gloucestershire, now led by a tough-as-teak centre from Kingsholm called John Bayliss, had seen off their regular rivals Lancashire in the semi-finals at Bristol during which John had come out well on top in the set piece against Colin Fisher who had just become the new hooker for Scotland. A mere week after the drubbing in Paris he was running out at Richmond's Athletic Ground to take part in a fine Championship Final victory over Middlesex due in no small part to the metronomic goal-kicking of full-back Peter Butler.

In April he had the unusual honour for an Englishman – albeit one who grew up as close to Wales as the River Severn would allow – to be selected for a Welsh President's team to celebrate the centenary of Abergavenny RFC on a Tuesday night only to play against Swansea the following evening back at Bristol. Hardly the behaviour of a man about to take things a bit easier.

No doubt flushed with the success of winning three County Championships and with no England or Lions tours in the offing, Gloucestershire embarked on a very ambitious tour to Southern Africa. This began in Salisbury against what was still named Rhodesia, then progressing by anything but easy stages to meet a North East Cape team at Graaff-Reinert, Eastern Province XV at Uitenhage near Port Elizabeth and taking in a South West team at George. They would then fly up onto the high veldt to take on the might of Northern Transvaal at Pretoria and Transvaal at Ellis Park in Johannesburg. This would all be rounded off by a trip to Windhoek in what is now known as Namibia – all in the space of three short weeks.

This would have been a gruelling enough itinerary for a full International team but for a County team – even one as battle hardened and 'savvy' as Gloucestershire – it was going to be extremely difficult. John was never under any illusions for it was the fourth time he had been out there on tour and knew precisely what to expect. His understudy as reserve hooker however was a young man named Fred Reed who had not long been in the Gloucester club team and was given in the match programmes as weighing a mere 13 stone. It was certainly going to be tough.

The County champions had done reasonably well against the lesser-rated teams but John's final return to Johannesburg (the scene of England's triumph four years earlier) was not a happy occasion as they were run off their feet by a powerful Transvaal team who racked up over fifty points in the process. Thus, his decade of foreign tours was to close on a somewhat downbeat manner.

The England selectors were now to turn their eyes elsewhere and the last two seasons of John's senior rugby career saw him once again more available to Bristol and his appearances were again much more regular. His hooking skills were as sharp as ever and he retains fond memories of taking a whole lot of scrums off Peter Wheeler when they clashed once again in a Bristol v Leicester match.

The Bristol captain at the time was winger Ken Plummer and he recalled having a quiet word with John before a key Cup match against Gloucester:

> It was a difficult moment for me as here was I – a mere winger and many years his junior – trying to tell a famous hooker who had been there and done everything (a celebrated British Lion and all of the rest) that I wanted to see a bit more out of him! I wasn't quite sure how he would take to being given the gee-up by someone like me but he seemed not to mind too much. We still got knocked out though.

The County team also did without John for a few matches but once more turned to him for the semi-final against Lancashire up at the picturesque Vale of Lune where Gloucestershire were pipped due to a string of penalty goals. This brought his County rugby to an end having by then appeared in no less than six County finals.

His last season was 1977/78 and was to be spent entirely with Bristol. Meanwhile the Lions had been out to New Zealand during the summer and Peter Wheeler had ousted Bobby Windsor for the hooking role in the Test team and had performed admirably aided and abetted by Fran Cotton and the self-evident talent of Graham Price. Ironically the Lions were leading 9-6 in the Final Test at

Auckland with only a few minutes to go and the chance to finish the series all square when Wheeler lost the ball in a tackle and it popped into the hands of a grateful Laurie Knight to clinch both the match and the series with an opportunist try.

The situation had changed back on the farm and for a while John was having to cope on his own. He had spent the early autumn playing in the United team but Guy Fawkes Day saw them due to travel down to Devon for a rather meaningless match at Newton Abbot. John was involved with the bonfire night in the village and, feeling slightly off colour, decided to cry off, which did not go down too well with the United team secretary. The following week's game was cancelled but the First team had a match a few miles up the road at Lydney.

The selection committee had decided to give a chance at hooker to a young ex-Weston-super-Mare player named Andy Whittle but John travelled as one of the two named replacements on the bench. Regentsholme in Lydney is not the most forgiving of places for anyone who might appear to be struggling and Whittle was being given a hard time of it. Inevitably he had to come off, at which point John went on in his place to declare it was one of the easiest games he could remember being in and Bristol ran out as 18-6 winners.

From then on John was back in the Bristol team for the rest of that final season. As it turned out Bristol had a generally good season which included a win over Llanelli and that 23-0 drubbing of Leicester and Peter Wheeler, which was to give John so much personal satisfaction. However, they had by then gone out of the John Player Cup in losing a tight quarter-final at Coventry.

The season and with it John's senior rugby-playing career were finally to end up at Gosforth on the north-east coast – the place he had travelled to in hope for his very first England Trial nearly thirteen years before. All the players from the Bristol team he had first played with way back in 1961 had long since retired, although there was one familiar face from the victorious Lions in the Gosforth back-row in Peter Dixon who was also soon to call it a day.

Typically, there were never any fanfares and at the time he had not actually made the decision that this particular match was going to be his last. His farming commitments and lack of cover had made him slightly conscious that he should try to avoid getting injured, which, as anybody who has played rugby well knows, greatly increases the risk of doing so. He knew better than anyone that with that worry in the back of his mind he could no longer give of his best and he had no wish to see his standards slip.

I knew that I had no interest in slipping down to play rugby at a lesser level for, much as I still loved the game, I knew instinctively that I would also be a target for every junior club's self-appointed 'hard case' who wanted to make a name for himself. I really didn't need that.

That year Brenda was also to present him with their third child, Joanne, and work on the farm was still unrelenting. When the summer came along and it was time to report back to Bristol for pre-season training his boots remained in the cupboard and he just stayed at home.

That autumn he would have reached the age of thirty-seven, he was still as strong and fit as ever, he had seen and done just about all there was to do in those days before World Cups and European trophies but the little man inside his head told him that was enough.

24

Looking Back and
a Life After Rugby

John was always up every morning without fail, summer or winter, at around five o'clock and off in his Land Rover to check on his sheep and on the farm in general. Then it was home for breakfast before going back out again to do all the heavy chores – enough to make many twenty-year-olds shudder.

Back for lunch and then off out again until around six o'clock when it was home for dinner and a bit of television before going out again last thing at around eleven to check everything was still as it should be. In the lambing season around late February to early April he would also be found up half the night to be with his ewes as they struggled to give birth. Given the fact that he was on his own and had around 400 of them, this was no mean feat.

In his time, he had picked up his fair share of injuries, bumps and stitches and of course that leg injury which ruined the 1973 Cup Final. Ironically his worst injury was nothing to do with rugby but was from being butted on the kneecap by an angry ram.

Unlike many of his contemporaries he sees plenty to admire in the professional game although he is naturally dismissive of modern-day scrummaging and the almost lost art of hooking. When asked what he would do if he was coming into the game now, his immediate response would be that he would simply have adapted to it. 'I learned to adapt then and I guess I'd learn to adapt now' was his laconic comment. He also states that he would have happily turned professional for a few years and taken the money that the Dylan Hartleys and Jamie Georges are now earning but would have gone straight back to his first love of farming as soon as it was time to hang up his boots. Several West Country front-row farmers made the transition to the paid ranks quite easily – Phil Vickery, Graham Dawe and Julian White spring to mind – and John feels he would have in all probability done the same.

Although he was never to play any more serious rugby he did take part in a few charity games including one over in Jersey where he linked up with his old mate Stack Stevens and did so again when the two of them journeyed all the way up to Melrose in the Scottish borders to play in a special match in aid of one of Frank Laidlaw's family.

He also became involved with a charity called CLIC when the young son of a local builder named Bob Woodward (who had done the extension to John and Brenda's house) fell terminally ill. John spent many hours with the boy and the friendship with the family continues long after the poor lad's untimely death. That charity linked up with a similar one under the name of Sir Malcolm Sargent, the famous conductor, and as CLIC Sargent provides support to the families of teenage cancer patients.

His friendship with Stack Stevens was to endure a lifetime and each summer for many years the Pullin family would spend a week down on his friend's farm deep in West Cornwall. Busy farmers seldom indulge in having holidays but there was always plenty of fun to be had when the two families got together.

Until he was laid low with the horrible disease that eventually claimed his life, Stevens was an incorrigible practical joker and a 'wind-up merchant' *par excellence*. There were plastic worms in the children's marmalade, dead fish hidden in cars, cellophane over loo seats and according to Robin Cowling, one night he had phoned up John's father Bill with a put-on voice to tell him that all his cows had been spotted heading over the Severn Bridge.

One summer Stack asked John and the family to stay on for an extra day for John and Brenda to act as witnesses when Stack was to marry a local girl named Jane Vingoe at a quiet wedding in nearby Helston. John was somewhat surprised to be asked and thought for a moment that it was yet another Stevens 'wind up'. When Jane later produced two sons herself, the two families were always travelling to the beach or playing cricket together, although John's family were of course by then quite a few years older but nevertheless they always had a great time together.

When Stack finally died in late 2017 it was John who led the tributes to a packed church in Penzance and Jonathan was one of the pall bearers. It was a very sad occasion but it followed some very happy times they had all enjoyed together.

John's father Bill passed away in 1994 but for some reason had left no will. This can often cause family problems but in this case the three brothers sat down and sorted it all out perfectly amicably between them. Indeed, the Pullins remain a very close-knit family, all living within easy reach of one another with Phillip living at Pear Tree Farm and in John and Brenda's case with their second daughter Joanne, who commutes from Aust to work for John Lewis at Cribb's Causeway, still living in the family home. Joanne has the courage to stand up and declare she has no interest in sport or farming for that matter.

As the son of a famous father, Jonathan also went to school in Thornbury, although like most around the country it was by then no longer a grammar school. He played all sports but soon turned to rugby. In time he became a very accomplished goal-kicker and in fact is still turning out for Thornbury RFC despite now being well into his forties.

He has played most of his rugby in the backs but was once persuaded to try being a hooker when he was a student at Hull University. He hated it and gave up the experiment after two or three games, so there was never any chance of too many comparisons ever being made. John never got involved with any coaching and was dissuaded from watching his son play too often as he seemed to be a bad omen as whenever he went along poor Jonathan seemed to get himself injured.

Jonathan has since carved out a very successful career not as a farmer as such but his life is closely aligned to the agricultural world. As a chartered surveyor he is the co-owner of a company called Voyce-Pullin, which values and sells farm properties and manages farm livestock auctions including running the widely used Cirencester market. His own son, Oscar, loves all sports that involve a ball.

His elder sister Mandy was mad on sport at school and desperately wanted to have been allowed to play rugby herself. Unfortunately, she was a few years ahead of her time for that but, as a professional sports instructor, she was an entrant for the TV show *Gladiators*, which she confirms is every bit as exhausting as it looks. She has also recently qualified as a driving instructor.

Because John always worked from his home the children saw far more of him than most children do their fathers and as soon as they were old enough they would come out with him onto the farm and were able to grow up naturally with calves and lambs all around them. He was never going to be a 'hands-on dad' in the sense of cooking or bathing them, and is doubtful if he had a clue how to change a nappy, but he was generally there to read them bedtime stories – although he sometimes used to cheat a bit and miss out a few pages if he was feeling particularly tired.

When he is able to relax and put his feet up his tastes are very much middle-of-the-road. His favourite singers are Elvis and Johnny Cash and pressed as to his favourite television programmes he recalls *Rising Damp* and *Dad's Army* as being the kind of thing he particularly liked. He also enjoys James Bond movies but unfortunately Brenda hates them, so he has to wait for them to be shown on TV. He also watches a fair bit of sport on television and apart from obviously rugby he has been very impressed with the commitment and team spirit shown by women hockey players.

It was mentioned earlier that John was a bit of a picky eater dating back to his early school days and the thing he always dreaded most when having to go into hospital for his various injuries was the almost universally revolting food he had to endure each time. Fortunately, both Brenda and Joanne are expert bakers and he enjoys good English cooking, although he is not averse to a curry or a Chinese occasionally. He also admits to a weakness for peppermints.

As with most independently minded farmers, John was never going to be one of those gin-and-tonic rugby committee men but perhaps surprisingly he served briefly for a couple of years on the committee of the Barbarians. He was never much of one for sitting in meetings but he discovered that it was not too arduous and mainly involved turning up for the traditional Easter Tour in South Wales and as he was at least thirty years younger than most of the other committee men he sometimes got pressed into touch-judge duties on their behalf.

Occasionally he would be asked whether he felt someone was the right sort of chap to represent the Baa-Baas, although when pressed he was not at all sure what qualified someone as being the 'right sort of chap' or not.

In the early days following his retirement from playing he attended a fair number of rugby-related dinners and reunions and actually returned to South Africa on the occasion of the South African Rugby Union's centenary, but these days is only very rarely seen – if ever – at Twickenham on International match days. Whilst compiling this book Tony Horton rounded up a party of the 1968 Lions and they returned to South Africa fifty years later but once again John's farm duties kept him at home. In point of fact his chief contact with the sport today is his continued loyal support of his first club Bristol Saracens.

Although Jonathan plays for Thornbury it is at the Saracens where John will turn out for annual dinners, awards nights and any other special functions which that thriving junior club wants to lay on. Naturally they love to have their most famous former player in attendance. According to Bristol Saracens stalwart Tony Swash, John never fails to make an appearance whenever asked and is held in high esteem by not only the old brigade but by the younger players as well. It is typical of John that he feels much closer to these grassroots players and officials than he ever would to the professional Bristol Bears and all their modern razzmatazz at Ashton Gate.

A few years ago, several of his friends from the Bristol Saracens got together some influential people including a couple of local MPs with a view to putting John's name forward for an OBE but nothing ever materialised. This seems particularly ironic when fringe members of England's 2003 World Cup-winning squad – some of whom had never played in a match or even sat on the bench – were all given MBEs.

No doubt he took this in his stride with just a shrug of his broad shoulders as he can look back over a close and happy family life, a stellar rugby career and, of course, as a dedicated livestock farmer.

However, let us finish by going back to the beginning with the Ireland v England match in 1973 and that short but moving speech. Rugby devotee and author Dave Fox recalled vividly an occasion just a few years ago as follows.

In the summer of 2013 Thornbury RFC celebrated its Golden Jubilee with a 'black tie' dinner. John Pullin was an honoured guest. The main speaker was Fergus Slattery, the truly great Irish flank forward and captain who had played for Ireland on that historic day in Dublin forty years before. In an electrifying moment of high emotion at the dinner, Slattery pointed to John and said,

> A great debt of gratitude is owed to that man. Scotland and Wales had pulled out of their games in Dublin and everyone expected England to do the same. But he led the England team to Dublin and stopped the 'contagion'. It was starting to affect business as well as sport and people and businesses were not coming to Ireland and it was beginning to have a marked effect on the economy. The contagion was spreading but he stopped it by bringing the England team to Dublin and honouring the fixture.

He then reiterated what we already know about that dinner in the Shelbourne Hotel after the game. 'When John Pullin stood up and his opening line was "We may not be very good but at least we turn up" he earned the respect of the Irish people.'

Respect! That is John Pullin the man: quiet, undemonstrative, strong, ruthlessly competitive, sometimes stubborn, highly accomplished but in the end a player and a man who still commands universal respect throughout the rugby world and beyond.

Senior Career Summary

Bristol: 296 matches (1st XV only) 11 tries
Debut: 9 Sep 1961 v Newport
Last match: 29 April 1978 v Gosforth

Gloucestershire: 48 matches including 6 County finals
Debut: 23 Oct 1965 v Somerset
Last match: 22 Jan 1977 v Lancashire

Barbarians: 19 matches including New Zealand match 1973
Debut: 8 Apr 1966 v Penarth
Last match: 27 Dec 1974 v Leicester
Committee member 1982–84

England: 42 matches including 13 as captain
Debut: 15 Jan 1966 v Wales
Last match: 20 Mar 1976 v France

British Lions: 27 matches including 7 Test matches
Debut: 22 May 1968 v Western Province
Last match: 14 Aug 1971 v New Zealand